KU-486-171

MANAGEMENT AND PRODUCTION

RAY WILD

PENGUIN BOOKS

Penguin Books Ltd, Harmondsworth, Middlesex, England
Penguin Books Inc., 7110 Ambassador Road, Baltimore, Maryland 21207, U.S.A.
Penguin Books Australia Ltd, Ringwood, Victoria, Australia

—

Published in Pelican Books 1972

—

Copyright © Ray Wild, 1972

—

Made and printed in Great Britain
by Richard Clay (The Chaucer Press), Ltd,
Bungay, Suffolk
Set in Monotype Times

This book is sold subject to the condition
that it shall not, by way of trade or otherwise
be lent, re-sold, hired out, or otherwise circulated
without the publisher's prior consent in any form of
binding or cover other than that in which it is
published and without a similar condition
including this condition being imposed
on the subsequent purchaser

Contents

CHAPTER 1

The Nature of Production

ECONOMISTS define production as the act of making something with the object of satisfying wants. Human wants are not, of course, confined solely to goods and commodities, but also include services; consequently the economist's definition of production is not restricted to the process of creating physical items. If one applies this definition a transportation system can be regarded as a production system, since its purpose is to convert items such as road vehicles or aircraft into a service. Similarly, the conversion of deposits into loans in the banking system can be considered as a production process, and a library or a hospital might be considered to be involved in the process of production.

Furthermore, even in a system concerned with the production of goods, wants are not satisfied until such goods are in the hands of the consumers, and consequently we might also consider the distribution or even the marketing process as part of the process of production. Certainly in many industries the marketing of products is a minor task in comparison with the task of physically creating such products; however, in other industries the process of marketing is of paramount importance and dominates the creating process.

For practical purposes it would seem that the definition of production provided by economists is too wide. Clearly production and marketing are separate yet interdependent functions in business, and there is little benefit in general in considering either one to be wholly contained by the other. Furthermore, in everyday usage the term production is normally associated with the assembly and provision of physical items rather than with the provision of services.

Production as a business function is concerned with conversion or transformation processes, but, as we have seen, such processes are not concerned exclusively with the provision of goods. Many

7

technologically diverse transformation processes exist in business; in the interests of clarity it is perhaps advisable to confine the term 'production' to those transformation processes concerned with the provision of goods, and use a term such as *operating systems* in referring to the wider classification of processes.

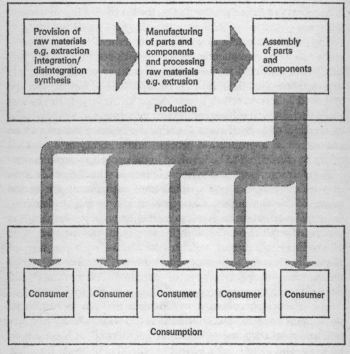

Figure 1

The assembly of motor cars is clearly a production process, as is the creation from raw materials of the parts such as pistons and springs which together constitute such vehicles. The fabrication of steel tanks is a production process, as is the process by which the steel plate was previously made from billets. Furthermore, the creation of raw materials, whether by extraction (e.g. steel), integration, (e.g. plastics), or disintegration (e.g. petroleum), is also a production process. Basically, therefore, production processes occur at three distinct levels: raw material provision, parts or component manufacture, and finally parts and components assembly. Often there occur several sequential steps at each of these levels but these three basic levels together constitute the total process of goods production (Figure 1).

PRODUCTION AND MANUFACTURE

A manufacturing system is concerned with the creation and provision of goods and as such the process of manufacture can be equated with the process of production as outlined above. A manufacturing or production system is concerned with the creation of physical outputs; in other words the conversion of materials and parts to goods or products. Such a process depends upon three basic components or physical resources – men, materials and machines – which are coordinated by means of plans and controls exercised by management.

Efficient manufacturing industries are of paramount importance to the economy of any developed nation. For example, the manufacturing industries in Great Britain employ 80 per cent of the active workforce, account for 34 per cent of the Gross National Product and provide 86 per cent of total exports.* In this country, as in the USA, engineering is by far the largest sector of the manufacturing industry, accounting for 85 per cent of manufactured exports and employing 27 per cent of the manufacturing labour force.

PRODUCTION AND OTHER BUSINESS FUNCTIONS

Production and marketing are the twin foundations of modern industry. The degree of 'overlap', the interdependence, and the nature of the cooperation between these functional areas depend,

* December 1969.

of course, upon the nature of the industry involved, or more directly upon the nature of the product being manufactured. There are undoubtedly situations in which marketing considera-

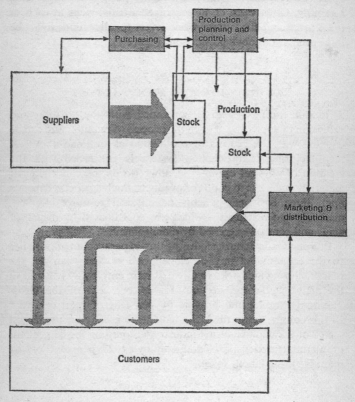

Figure 2

tions dominate production and vice versa, but in general the interrelation between the two functions is wide and encompasses such things as demand forecasting, stock-holding policies, production rate determination and scheduling (Figure 2).

In addition to this important interrelation the production

10

function in any business inevitably and necessarily overlaps with finance, design and development, purchasing and personnel departments, as follows:

Production/Purchasing

Maintenance of stocks of materials purchased, equipment and various indirect items
Quality control of incoming items
Provision of purchase prices for estimation purposes

Production/Finance

Provision of operation times for cost and wage calculation
Preparation of production budgets
Equipment replacement decisions
Production estimates

Production/Marketing

Demand forecasting
Production scheduling to satisfy delivery dates
Capacity planning
Progress information

Production/Design and Development

Design of new products
Manufacture of prototypes
Modifications to existing products
Manufacturing standards and quality determination
Equipment design

Production/Personnel

Labour recruitment and selection
Training
Industrial relations
Incentive payment
Safety and health
Welfare

11

THE TYPES OF PRODUCTION

The production process at the two final levels – raw material processing and the assembly of items into products – can be classified into certain further levels depending upon the scale of operations, or more particularly upon the degree of repetitiveness in production. There are, of course, two extremes to this scale of repetitiveness: *unique production* in which there is absolutely no repetition, each product being different; and *continuous production* in which all products are identical. Pure forms of these two types of production are difficult to envisage; however, civil engineering is perhaps the best (although rather special) example of the former, whilst petroleum refining is a good but not perfect example of the latter.

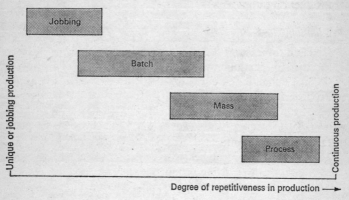

Figure 3

Between these two limits there exists a very wide gulf into which fits almost all of the world's manufacturing activities. Since this whole area between the two extremes is characterized by the production of items neither in single quantities nor continuously, it might be referred to as *batch production*; however this description is normally confined to production approaching the unique limit, whilst the term *mass production* is used to describe production which is almost continuous or continuous over a limited but substantial period of time.

A further term, *process production*, is often used to describe continuous production by means of chemical or bulk processes, whilst mass production is normally used in referring to repetitive production of individual items such as motor cars.

These four principal types of production (Figure 3) are not of course the only means of categorizing production processes. Drucker* initially identifies three types, unique product, mass and process, but later goes on to add a fourth type by dividing mass production into mass production 'old style', that is 'the production of uniform products', and mass production 'new style', which is concerned with the manufacture of uniform parts and their assembly into diversified products. Falk† identifies three types of production which he describes as follows:

Process production	Continuous flow production
	Process production of chemicals in batches
	Process production combined with the preparation of a product for sale by large batch or mass production methods
Large-batch and mass production	Mass production
	Production of large batches
	Production of components in large batches subsequently assembled diversely
Small-batch and unit production	Production of small batches
	Fabrication of large equipments in stages
	Manufacture of technically complex unit articles
	Manufacture of simple unit articles to customer order

* Peter F. Drucker, *The Practice of Management*, Heinemann, 1955.
† Roger Falk, *The Business of Management*, Pelican, 1961.

One further dimension by which production processes may be classified derives from the nature of the production planning function. If product specifications can only be determined by direct contact with the individual customer, then products will be made *to individual customer order*. If, however, product specifications can be determined in advance without direct contact with individual customers, products can be *made for stock, in anticipation of customer orders*.

The classification of production processes using any of the above systems is clearly a somewhat artificial and often arbitrary procedure, but as a preliminary to discussing the management of production it is essential, because each type of production makes its own demands on all aspects of the management of the business.

The management problems associated with each of the classes of production will be discussed in detail in the next chapter, and for the remainder of this chapter we shall be concerned with one important feature associated with the type of production – the nature of the layout of the manufacturing facilities.

There are three basic types of layout:

Layout by Fixed Position

Here the product remains stationary, and the facilities required during its manufacture are brought to it as and when required.

Layout by Process

Here facilities of a similar type or purpose are located together and products move between the groups of equipment according to the order of operations required to be performed on the product.

Layout by Product

Here the facilities are arranged according to the manufacturing needs of the product.

The appropriateness of each of these types of layout for each type of production is illustrated in Figure 4.

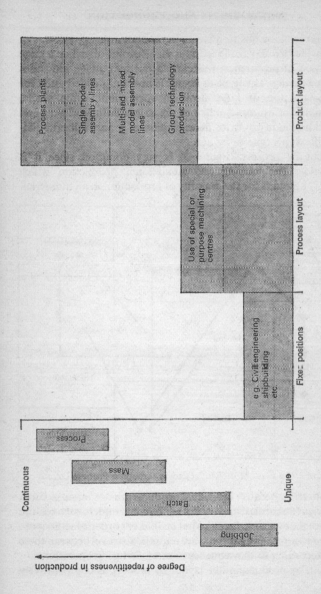

Figure 4 Degree of Specialization of Layout

Layout by fixed position is rare in modern industry but was of course widespread before the Industrial Revolution, when a large proportion of production was carried out by cottage industries such as weaving. This type of layout is now only widely used for the manufacture of large items in very small, often single, quantities. For example, much of the shipbuilding industry and the building industry, with the exception of industrialized building, utilizes this type of layout.

Layout by process (Figure 5) is very common since it is appropriate for jobbing and small-batch production which probably accounts for the majority of production in all industrial-

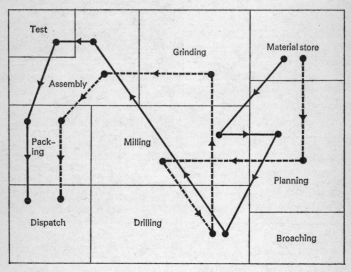

Figure 5 The Flow of Individual Orders through a Process Layout

ized countries. Because individual products are not manufactured in sufficient quantities, and because different products each require the use of the available facilities but in different orders, facilities are grouped together and products are required to travel between these areas, according to the sequence of manufacturing operations.

Layout by product, unlike layout by process, is comparatively

16

inflexible since the facilities are arranged in a manner dictated by the manufacturing requirements of the product. The demand for the product must be sufficiently high to enable the facilities, normally arranged in the form of a flow assembly line (Figure 6), to be fully utilized, since idle time on the facilities cannot readily be utilized in the manufacture of other products which probably require different operations in a different order.

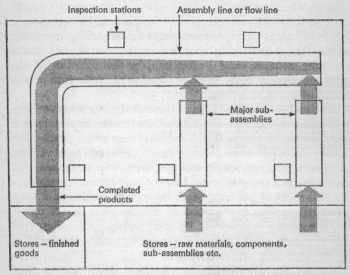

Figure 6 The Assembly of Identical Products by Means of a Product Manufacturing Layout

It is unusual for any organization to depend solely upon any one of these three types of layout. Even in a mass-production industry there is normally a need to manufacture certain items, such as jigs or tools, in small quantities. In batch production products often incorporate similar or identical components which because of combined demand might be appropriate for manufacture by methods more usually associated with mass production industries.

Because of technological developments in the design of manufacturing facilities, and the adoption of new production management techniques, the overlap between the 'classic' types of layout, particularly layouts by process and product, is continually increasing, and nowadays it is common to find product type layouts in batch or even jobbing production industries. In fact, in this respect two developments are worth noting. Firstly, a feature noted by Drucker, the use of similar or identical parts or components in a diversity of products; because of such design rationalization many companies have been able to adopt mass production techniques in parts or component manufacture. Furthermore, it has been found that it is not necessary to produce large quantities of identical parts to adopt more efficient semi-continuous manufacturing methods, since it often happens that sufficient similar parts are required in the batch production of products to permit a type of layout of facilities.*

A second development of importance is the increasing need for companies engaged in mass production to offer to customers a wide range of products. It is, for example, no longer possible for companies in the motor industry to offer only one basic vehicle, since customers now seek a choice of style, trim, equipment and finish. There is therefore a need for such companies to manufacture a variety of products based on a common design, a need which is usually accomplished by the use of multi- or mixed model assembly or flow lines. (In other words, by the adjustment of the 'classic' mass production type of layout to accommodate batch production requirements.)

Finally, the influence of technological developments is of course vitally important. In particular, over the past four or five years the increasing use of numerically controlled machine tools and complex machining centres has begun to transform traditional batch production, and process layouts are being replaced or supplemented by programmed batch production machining centres consisting of one complex facility.

READING REFERENCE

Timms, H. L., *The Production Function in Business*, Irwin, 1967.

* This type of manufacture is known as Group Technology, or Family Parts Machining.

CHAPTER 2

The Nature of Production Management

THE NATURE OF MANAGEMENT

ECONOMISTS define the factors or agents of production as land, labour, and resources. Use of the terms factor or agent in this connection is, however, somewhat misleading since both seem to imply the playing of an active part. Clearly these three things in combination do somehow provide the wealth of nations, but only when brought together in the presence of an organizing authority or catalyst. This catalyst is, of course, management, and the three factors of production are the resources or inputs at the disposal of management.

The Manager is the dynamic, life-giving element in every business. Without his leadership 'the resources of production' remain resources and never become production. In a competitive economy, above all, the quality and performance of the managers determine the success of a business, indeed they determine its survival. For the quality, and performance of its managers is the only effective advantage an enterprise in a competitive economy can have.

In this rather passionate description of management Drucker* recognizes the catalytic role of management in relation to the resources of production.

Clearly the practice of management involves decision-making, the devising of plans and strategies and the general utilization of resources in the most effective manner with respect to the objectives of the company or body concerned. In general, therefore, management can be defined as the function of governing, involving the determination and coordination of the activities of the company.

Organization is the instrument of management, the vehicle created with the purpose of assisting management to fulfil its

* Peter F. Drucker, *The Practice of Management*, Heinemann, 1955.

19

objectives. The process of organizing invariably involves a manager in dealing with other people; indeed one of the major tasks of management (often one of the major problems) concerns the organizational relationships with other people. Notice, however, that such a task is only a consequence and not the purpose of management. Certainly dealing with subordinates, superiors, and peers is a crucial aspect of the manager's job, but it is normally only an instrumental activity. This activity of management has often been confused with the objective or purpose of management, a situation which has sometimes led to the use of misleading definitions such as 'Management means getting other people to do the things one wants them to do'* and 'Management is the practice of deciding for others (the managed) the use of all resources, and getting others to implement these decisions.'† Certainly such definitions do serve to emphasize one of the most important problem areas of management, but even in this particular context their emphasis on enforcement suggests the existence of an undesirable relationship between the manager and other members of his organization. In this context it is worth noting that dictionary definitions of management often refer to 'trickery' and 'deceitful contrivance'.‡

The management process consists basically of four stages:

(1) *Establish Objectives*

This is a prerequisite for any planning or control activities. In certain cases, objectives may be established for a manager by a superior or indeed a customer. The determination of objectives will usually involve management in:

Gathering data
Converting data into pertinent information
Establishing alternative objectives
Evaluating objectives
Deciding amongst alternatives

* *Works Management in Practice*, ed. R. R. Gilchrist, Heinemann, 1970.
† Howard L. Timms, *Introduction to Operations Management*, Irwin, 1967.
‡ See *Oxford Concise Dictionary*.

(2) *Determine Activities Necessary to Achieve Objectives*

This will normally involve management in planning work, usually the work of others, and in dividing this work amongst the resources available. Depending upon the nature of the objectives, these planning operations may occur in two stages: long term planning – strategic planning concerned with the establishment of an overall situation within which objectives might be pursued, and short-term planning – tactical planning concerned with shorter-term decision-making.

(3) *Control*

This should verify that the plans previously established are working satisfactorily and are having the desired effect. This step may incorporate a certain amount of contingency planning and will certainly involve considerable man-management tasks.

(4) *Measurement of Results*

The final stage is naturally concerned with an evaluation of the success of the previous three stages. Information gathered during this stage will quite likely affect decision-making in stages 1, 2 and 3 on occasions in the future.

This evaluation of the management process is of course highly abstract, and few managers will operate within such a formal sequential process. In practice, at any one time most managers are likely, because of the extent of their responsibilities, to be concerned with numerous problems all at different stages. Moreover, they are likely also to be involved in a host of instrumental activities designed to assist in the achievement of specific and general objectives. For example, a manager's responsibilities to his subordinates will involve him in motivating individuals, delegating both responsibility and authority, developing abilities, and assessing performance and progress. In addition the manager will be required to cooperate with both equals in other functions and superiors on matters involving past, present, and future operations.

MANAGEMENT FUNCTIONS

Managerial responsibility within any organization is normally defined loosely by means of a hierarchical structure of the type shown in Figure 7. The various horizontal levels correspond to various levels of responsibility and authority whilst the vertical

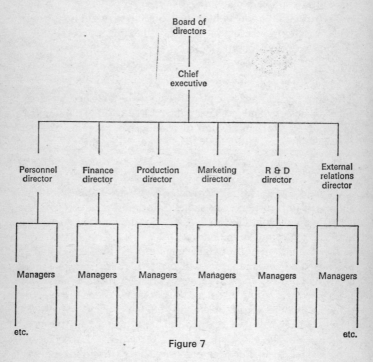

Figure 7

divisions correspond to specialist or functional responsibilities and authority. This hierarchical representation is of value only as an approximate representation of company organization, since various features not represented on such diagrams usually complicate both the organizational design and, more particularly, organizational practice. In particular, one must distinguish

22

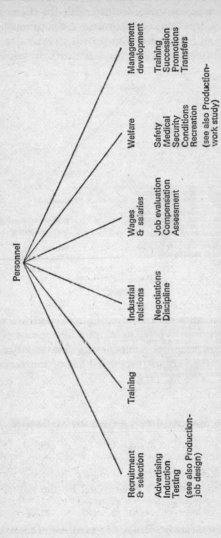

Personnel

Recruitment & selection
Advertising
Induction
Testing
(see also Production–job design)

Training

Industrial relations
Negotiations
Discipline

Wages & salaries
Job evaluation
Compensation
Assessment

Welfare
Safety
Medical
Security
Conditions
Recreation
(see also Production–work study)

Management development
Training
Succession
Promotions
Transfers

Figure 8

between line management (concerned with the direct management of the basic functions of the company, e.g. production), and staff management (concerned with providing specialist services, advice and information to line management). In addition it is

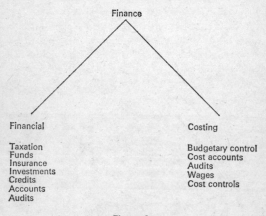

Finance

Financial

Taxation
Funds
Insurance
Investments
Credits
Accounts
Audits

Costing

Budgetary control
Cost accounts
Audits
Wages
Cost controls

Figure 9

necessary to recognize the existence of informal as well as formal organization, the former often developing as a means of complementing, extending, and/or compensating for the latter. Figures 8 to 13 outline the various responsibilities of the various functions.*

THE MANAGEMENT OF PRODUCTION

The nature of production management is, of course, determined by the nature of the production system. Not only the difficulty of the problems facing production managers but their very nature and existence are inevitably determined by the nature and the characteristics of the production system.

* These descriptions are intended to be typical, but of course the details of any organization will depend upon the circumstances.

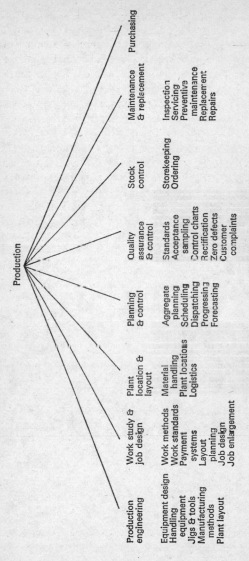

Production

Production engineering	Work study & job design	Plant location & layout	Planning & control	Quality assurance & control	Stock control	Maintenance & replacement	Purchasing
Equipment design	Work methods	Material handling	Aggregate planning	Standards	Storekeeping	Inspection	
Handling equipment	Work standards	Plant locations	Scheduling	Acceptance sampling	Ordering	Servicing	
Jigs & tools	Payment systems	Logistics	Dispatching	Control charts		Preventive maintenance	
Manufacturing methods	Layout planning		Progressing	Rectification		Replacement	
Plant layout	Job design		Forecasting	Zero defects		Repairs	
	Job enlargement			Customer complaints			

Figure 10

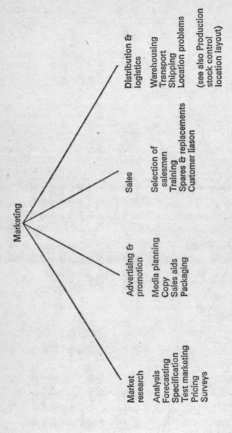

Figure 11

In abstract terms, the objectives of production management are firstly the design and secondly the operation of production systems, i.e. the design of a system incorporating labour,

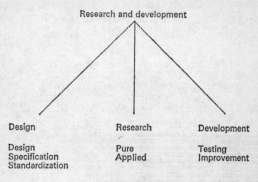

Figure 12

materials, and machines and the operation of such a system, according to a suitable plan or organization.

In passing it is worth noting that a production or manufactur-

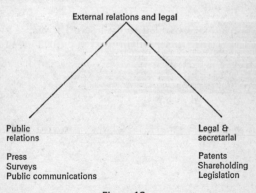

Figure 13

ing system is an *operating system*. In fact the process of production or manufacture is the principal type of operating system, other types being distribution or logistic systems, transportation,

27

and other non-manufacturing systems such as hospitals, libraries etc. Although much of what we shall deal with in this book will be of relevance to operating systems as a whole, we are concerned primarily with production management rather than operations management, since we are dealing with manufacture, or the production of goods rather than services.

PRODUCTION MANAGEMENT PROBLEM AREAS

The production function can normally be described in terms of eight components (Figure 10):

(1) Production engineering
(2) Work study and job design
(3) Plant location and layout
(4) Production planning and control
(5) Quality control
(6) Stock control
(7) Maintenance and replacement
(8) Purchasing

This list might be extended to include other items, the responsibility for which rests partly within the production function, e.g.:

(9) Product design
(10) Payment and incentives

Alternatively, the original list might be shortened by the omission of 8 (Purchasing), which is often associated with the marketing function or exists quite separately.

(1) *Production Engineering*

'A production engineer is one who is competent by reason of education, training and experience in technology and management to determine the factors involved in the manufacture of commodities, and to direct the productive process to achieve the most efficient coordination of effort, with due respect to quantity, quality and cost.' This definition given by the Institution of Production Engineers* is of comparatively little value in determining the problems associated with this function, except that it indicates that production engineers are concerned with manufacture rather than with the broader definition of production.

In many respects the relationship between production engineering and production management is typical of that existing between the business professions and management. Production engineering is a well-defined, comparatively long-established and recognized profession, organized by a professional body incorporated in 1931. There are formal and recognized educational requirements for membership of the profession and long-established under- and post-graduate courses available. In comparison production management is an ill-defined area of responsibility as yet unrecognized as a profession and an educational subject. It is perhaps because of this relationship that, although production engineering is undoubtedly one area of responsibility of production management, the former rarely constitutes part of the syllabus during the teaching of the latter. The scope of production engineering inferred by the above description is, no doubt deliberately, rather broad, since in practice the production engineer, working as an engineer and not as a manager, would normally be concerned predominantly with the design and operation of the production facilities rather than with the direction of the production process or system. In other words, the production engineer will normally be concerned with one of the four aspects of a production system. The relationship between the engineer and the manager with respect to production is illustrated in Figure 14.

Because of the separate identity and the scope of production engineering we shall not attempt to deal with the subject in the limited space available here.

* *Practical Training in Production Engineering*, I. Prod. E., 1961.

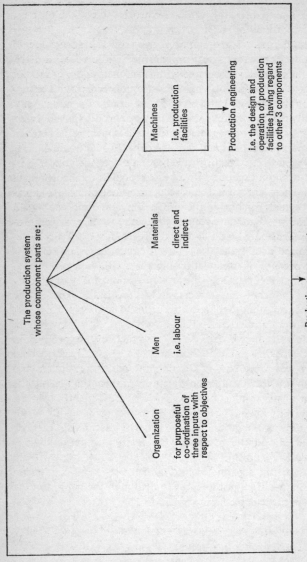

The production system
whose component parts are:

Organization	Men	Materials	Machines
for purposeful co-ordination of three inputs with respect to objectives	i.e. labour	direct and indirect	i.e. production facilities

Production engineering

i.e. the design and operation of production facilities having regard to other 3 components

Production management

i.e. the design and operation of the production process

Figure 14

(2) *Work Study and Job Design*

Work study, or *time and motion study*, as it is more frequently called in America, derives directly from the scientific management movement and the pioneering work of Taylor, Gilbreth, Bedeaux and others. It is a crucial aspect of production management, not only because of its historical place in the development of the subject, but mainly because it is concerned with two common denominators of production systems, work methods and work measurement.

The British Standards Institution defines work study as 'a generic term for those techniques, particularly method study and work measurement, which are used in the examination of human work in all its contexts, and which lead systematically to the investigation of all the factors which affect the efficiency and economy of the situation being reviewed, in order to effect improvement' (BS 3138).

In principle, work study is concerned with:

Human manual work
Determining efficient work methods
Determining standards of performance

Work study is essentially a short-term management technique. It is concerned with the improvement of productivity in existing jobs, and the maximization of productivity in the design of new jobs, within the limitations imposed by existing circumstances.

Method study, one of the two principal components of work study, is defined (BS 3138) as 'The systematic recording and critical examination of existing and proposed ways of doing work, as a means of developing and applying easier and more effective methods and reducing costs'. Efficient work methods are clearly of paramount importance in production. The standardization of efficient methods is, of course, an adequate objective itself, but the application of method study might also give rise to one or more of the following benefits:

Improved work environment
Improved facilities layout

31

Better utilization of equipment
Improved safety
Better materials handling
Better production flow and less work in progress
Better wages

Work measurement is defined (BS 3138) as 'the application of techniques designed to establish the time for a qualified worker to carry out a specified job at a defined level of performance'. Work measurement logically follows method study as follows:

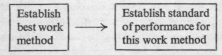

Notice, however, that during method study the quantitative data provided by work measurement may be necessary in evaluating alternative work methods. The determination of work standards is often associated with the design and use of incentive payment systems. This is undoubtedly a major application of work measurement data, but should not be the sole justification for a work measurement programme, since work standards will also be required for:

Production scheduling
Manpower planning
Cost estimating
Maintenance planning

The various steps involved in conducting both method study and work measurement exercises are shown in Figure 15. The figure also indicates the alternative work measurement techniques which are available and shows how work standards are used in determining and installing efficient work methods.

Work, of course, is only one part of any job, since the latter also embraces social relations, the payment system, working conditions, supervisory arrangements etc. It is only comparatively recently that the importance of job design has been recognized, and it is still not fully accepted that the simple application of

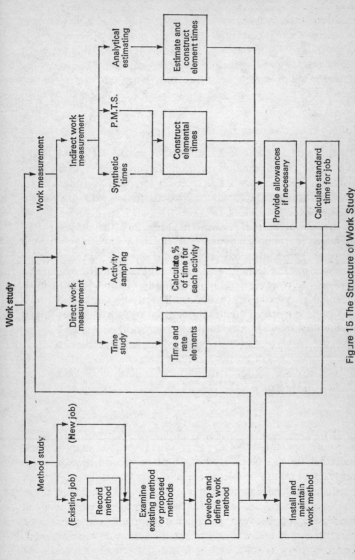

Figure 15 The Structure of Work Study

Reproduced by permission from R. Wild, *The Techniques of Production Management*, Holt Rinehart & Winston, 1970.

traditional work study principles is only one part of a far larger problem. There is currently a great deal of discussion concerning the problems of job design; nevertheless it is clear that the work study practitioner has an important responsibility in job design, a responsibility which must be complemented by that of behavioural scientists representing the personnel function.

(3) Plant Location and Layout

The problem of locational choice does not lie solely within the province of the production function, and although it occurs comparatively infrequently, it is a crucially important problem which involves most of the functions or departments within the company, production included.

The layout of the physical facilities and the movement of materials is an important aspect of the design of any production process. The traditional methods of layout planning derive largely from the techniques of method study, and in particular some of the recording techniques used in method study form an essential part of layout planning. The design and selection of appropriate materials handling equipment is a problem falling predominantly within the field of production engineering; however the movement requirements of materials and parts is an important aspect of layout planning since the principal objective of any facilities layout is usually the minimization of the total cost of movement.

(4) Production Planning and Control

Planning and control is the heart of production management; indeed the problems of production planning and control are so important that this problem area is often considered to constitute production management.

There is a good deal of confusion concerning the meaning and the distinction between production planning and production control. In this text we shall adopt the following general definitions:

PRODUCTION PLANNING is the determination, acquisition, and arrangement of all facilities necessary for future production of items. In other words production planning is essentially a pre-production activity, associated with the design of the production system. The production system is considered to incorporate an organizational element in addition to physical facilities, and production planning is concerned with organizing the production of an item prior to the commencement of production.

It is helpful to consider production planning under two headings:

(1) *Long/medium-term planning* is concerned with the acquisition and arrangement of facilities for future production without reference to the production requirement or plans for individual items. This aspect of production planning is often called aggregate planning since it is concerned with aggregate production units. The inputs at this stage of planning are the sales forecast and the long-term corporate company policy.

(2) *Short-term production planning* or *scheduling* is concerned with the details of the production of individual items or orders. The principal characteristic of this stage of production planning is the construction of schedules which show the starting dates for each operation or each stage in the manufacture of items or orders.

PRODUCTION CONTROL is the corollary to short-term production planning or scheduling, and is quite simply concerned with the implementation of production schedules. Production control goes on during production and consists essentially of the following steps:

Initiating production
Dispatching of items (i.e. establishing priorities between items competing for time on the same facility)
Progressing
Reporting back to production planning

The importance and the difficulties associated with both planning and control depend essentially upon the nature of the production system. For example, in a mass production industry the (few) products will each flow through the stages of a well-defined production process. Investment in equipment will be high, and the flexibility of the process will be low, consequently it is important that a sufficiently high demand is maintained to provide for the full utilization of equipment. In other words demand forecasting and production planning are of considerable importance, whereas production control is a comparatively routine matter since, because of the inflexible specialized nature of the process, production will be continuous, almost automatic, and comparatively few unpredictable events will occur. In comparison, in jobbing production, because of the considerable variety of products (often being manufactured for the first time), considerable flexibility must be provided, large work in progress stocks will occur, queues of jobs will pile up and as a result accurate production planning is often impossible and production control is both difficult and crucial.

(5) Quality Control and Assurance

The reliability of a product in use is closely associated with its quality. The 'potential' reliability of a product on delivery to the customer is a function of both the design and the manufacture of the product. In fact a product is 'invested' with quality and reliability during design, as a result of the specifications adopted, and during manufacture as a result of the degree to which manufacture conforms to the design specifications (Figure 16).

The specifications, in terms of materials, dimensional tolerances etc., determined during the design stage, will of course have been influenced to some extent by production considerations, and not least by the characteristics of the available production facilities. This overlap between the design and the production functions is an essential one in determining and providing product quality, but the principal responsibility of the production manager in this respect concerns manufacture quality. The purpose of quality control and assurance is to ensure, if possible, that all items and products leaving the company conform to the declared specifications.

The principal problem in designing quality control and assurance procedures is to obtain a satisfactory balance between the cost of the procedure and the cost of producing defective items.

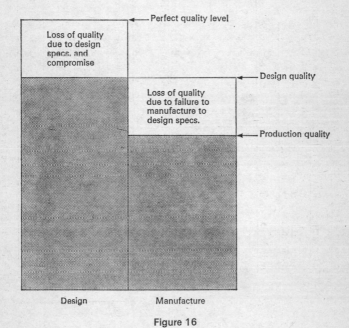

Figure 16

In practice, except in special circumstances, the cost associated with inspecting every item produced is not justified by the potential benefits, consequently quality control and assurance procedures normally depend upon random sampling techniques.

A total quality control and assurance procedure can be considered to consist of three stages, the purposes of which are shown in Figure 17.

37

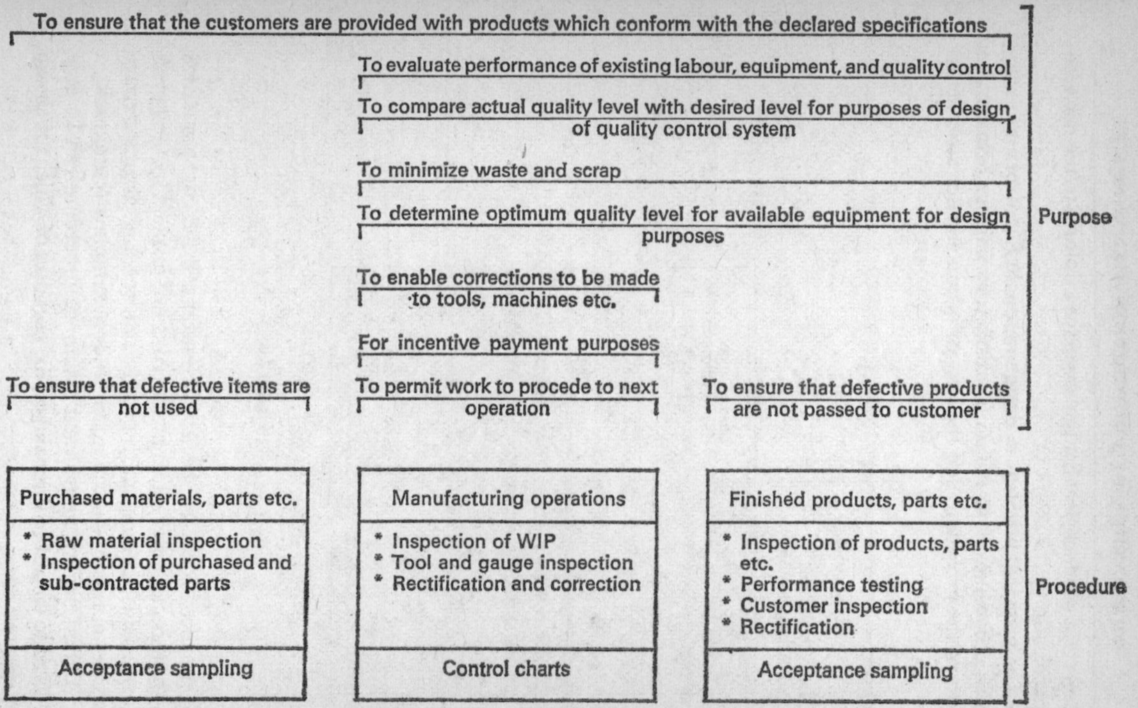

Figure 17 The Procedures and Purposes of Quality Control

Reproduced by permission from R. Wild, *The Techniques of Production Management*, Holt, Rinehart & Winston, 1970.

(6) *Stock or Inventory Control*

The purposes of stock or inventory are as follows:

(1) STOCKS OF FINISHED ITEMS:

To act as a buffer against fluctuations in demand for a product. Fluctuations in demand cannot normally be predicted with any degree of accuracy, however, even if such fluctuations could be predicted, it is often undesirable or inconvenient to accommodate them by corresponding fluctuations in the level of production. Consequently stocks of finished items are often maintained in order to permit a reasonably level production rate in the face of a fluctuating demand (see Figure 18).

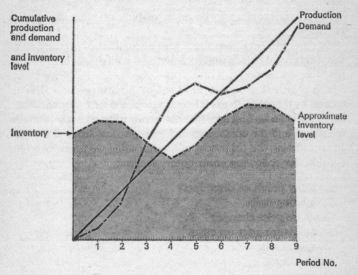

Figure 18 The Use of Inventory to Permit Level Production Rate in Face of Fluctuating Demand

To provide a quick service to the customer, i.e. to enable the customer's demand to be fulfilled almost immediately, rather than asking him to wait until an item is manufactured specifically for him.

39

To reduce the risk associated with stoppages or reductions in production caused by breakdowns, strikes, shortages of materials etc.

(2) WORK IN PROGRESS: stocks of components and partly completed items:

To disconnect or decouple the various stages of production thus facilitating production planning and enabling fluctuation in output at successive stages to occur without immediately affecting other stages. This decoupling process might also enable the production rates at successive stages to be stabilized.

(3) STOCK OF RAW MATERIALS AND PURCHASED ITEMS:

To enable advantages to be taken of bulk or other favourable purchasing terms.

To reduce the risk associated with disruptions of production at suppliers and to reduce the risk associated with delays in deliveries for other reasons.

The principal objective in stock or inventory control is of course, to minimize the total costs associated with stockholding, i.e. to obtain a satisfactory balance between the cost of maintaining stocks and the cost associated with possible stock shortages. In considering the total cost of stockholding we must therefore consider the following contributory factors:

Quantity purchase discounts
Purchasing costs
Purchase price changes
Manufacturing set-up costs
Wastage costs
Labour costs
Deterioration costs
Obsolescence costs
Insurance and storage costs
Notional loss of interest on tied-up capital
Costs of stockouts
Costs of fluctuations in production levels

The specific decisions required in maintaining effective stock control are as follows:

To what extent shall each item (raw material, products etc.) be controlled, i.e. how tightly shall control be exercised for each item?

With respect to each item: when shall a purchase or manufacturing order be placed?

With respect to each item: what quantity shall constitute a purchase or manufacturing order?

(7) *Maintenance and Replacement*

The objective of equipment maintenance is the maximization of the performance of production facilities by attempting to prevent breakdowns, and minimizing the loss or inconvenience caused by unavoidable breakdowns. The purpose of maintenance, therefore, is to improve the reliability of equipment, and as such maintenance can be seen as one part of a larger process concerned with reliability assurance as shown in Figure 19.

Objective	Equipment design	Equipment manufacture	Use and arrangement of equipment	Equipment maintenance and repair
(1) To attempt to ensure that breakdowns do not occur	Improved design standards	Improved quality control and assurance		Preventive maintenance
(2) To attempt to minimize the cost of breakdowns	Design to facilitate repair		Layout of equipment to facilitate repair Provide excess production capacity Use work in progress to 'decouple' facilities	Establish repair facility

Figure 19

Preventive maintenance is an important aspect of reliability assurance, and consists essentially of two aspects. Firstly, inspection of equipment in order to attempt to diagnose impending failure, and secondly servicing to reduce wear and hence attempt to prevent or delay breakdowns. The principal problem in planning preventive maintenance is that of determining when a piece of equipment should receive attention. Ideally one would wish to apply preventive maintenance just before a piece of equipment would otherwise have broken down. However, advance warning of breakdown is rarely available, consequently the timing of preventive maintenance must result from a statistical study of the probability distribution of breakdowns, usually obtained from historical operating data.

One of the principal problems in establishing a repair facility is the determination of the size of the repair team or 'gang'. This decision will be influenced by the costs associated with machine-down time and repair facility idle time, as well as the number of machines to be attended by the repair team, and their statistical reliability characteristics.

Problems of replacement are basically financial investment decisions. For example, the decision as to whether or not to replace an ageing machine with a new piece of equipment will depend upon a comparison of two aspects for both the present and the proposed machine: investment required, present and future, and revenues created by the machines with respect to time. A further common type of replacement problem concerns that of group replacement policies, i.e. given the existence in operation of several identical objects (e.g. light bulbs) whether to replace each object individually on failure, replace all objects collectively on the failure of any one, or replace certain but not all objects on the failure of one. Here the problem of designing a replacement policy will depend upon the expected life of the items, the number of items, their cost, and the cost of individual and group replacement.

(8) *Purchasing*

The status of the purchasing department within the company and its relation to the production function will depend largely upon the proportion of the total cost of the manufactured product(s) accounted for by 'bought-out' items, such as raw materials, components and indirect materials.

Because the purchasing department is often a separately accountable area of operations, or sometimes a part of the marketing department, we shall not consider these operations in any detail in this text. However, in passing it is worth emphasizing the extent and the nature of the overlap and interdependence of the purchasing department and the general production function.

This overlap may be summarized as follows:

The need to maintain adequate stocks of raw materials, components and indirect materials (see 6. *Stock control*)

The need to ensure that bought-out items conform to the design specification (see 5. *Quality control and assurance*)

The need to provide delivery times and purchase prices for estimating and quoting product costs and deliveries

The need to continually seek improved purchasing terms and in particular to inform both production and design and development of the availability of new and improved materials, etc.

Other Problem Areas

For reasons of space, we must confine the discussion in the following chapters to the principal features and problems of production management as listed above. It should, however, be noted that the list is by no means exhaustive. Certain problems fall between the eight areas mentioned and others have been omitted entirely. However, we have provided an adequate framework upon which to discuss most, if not all, of the important aspects of production management.

THE CLASSIFICATION OF PROBLEM AREAS
AND METHODS

Classification of Problem Areas

In this chapter we have defined production management as being concerned with the design and operation of production systems. In the later chapters we shall look at the use of quantitative and qualitative methods in both of these fields of production management. It may therefore be of value, before going into details about the various methods, to place each of the problem areas we have just discussed into the appropriate class. Any such classification must be to some extent arbitrary, but the following classification will form the basis for our subsequent discussion:

THE DESIGN OF PRODUCTION SYSTEMS

Work study and job design
Plant location and layout
Production planning (including forecasting)

THE OPERATION OF PRODUCTION SYSTEMS

Stock control
Quality control and assurance
Production control
Maintenance and replacement

Classification of Methods

No management decision is likely to be based entirely on either quantitative or qualitative reasoning. Even the most subjective management judgements are likely to be based on a certain, perhaps very small, amount of quantitative information. Similarly no important management decisions will be based exclusively on quantitative analysis because even in the simplest situation there are likely to be factors which defy quantification. We must, however, distinguish between decisions and methods of decision making. In making a decision we are concerned with the evaluation of alternative courses of action using whatever relevant data is available. The methods with which we deal with this data may vary, indeed decisions may well be based upon the results of several complementary evaluational methods, and such methods may vary from the entirely quantitative to the entirely qualitative. In Chapters 3–6 of this book we have categorized such methods as mathematical and qualitative and heuristic.

| | Mathematical methods | | Qualitative and heuristic methods Chapter 6 |
	Design of systems Chapter 4	Operation of systems Chapter 5	
Work study and job design		✕	Work study
Plant location and layout	Plant location Plant layout	✕	Plant layout
Production planning and control	Forecasting Aggregate planning Scheduling Assignment	Production control	Resource allocation Design of assembly lines Dispatching
Quality assurance and control	✕	Quality assurance Quality control	
Stock control	✕	Stock control	
Maintenance and replacement	✕	Maintenance Replacement	

Figure 20

This classification has been adopted largely for reasons of convenience and it is certainly not intended to be either a rigorous or an exclusive classification. In Chapters 3–5, dealing with mathematical methods, we will be concerned with methods of treating data, and of providing information for decision making which rely on a predominantly mathematical approach. We shall describe methods derived from mathematics and statistics and techniques developed by operational research workers and management scientists. The methods and techniques described in these chapters are not exclusively methods of optimizing, since the decision to include materials in these chapters has depended solely upon the mathematical emphasis, i.e. whether or not mathematical or statistical analysis forms a major part of the method. Nevertheless by this criterion most of the methods described are optimizing methods.

Chapter 6, dealing with qualitative and heuristic methods, contains descriptions of methods which are either entirely or predominantly non-mathematical in the terms described above, or heuristic, i.e. based on intuitive logic which does not necessarily lead to optimal solutions. Such methods are of considerable importance in production management since the complexity of many problems precludes a more rigorous approach. Superficially, heuristic methods bear some resemblance to traditional mathematical methods, since both involve the use of figures. It should, however, be noticed that heuristic procedures derive initially from intuitive reasoning and usually constitute simple rules or procedures which if applied consistently *have been found to provide satisfactorily good* but not necessarily optimum results. To facilitate reference the table shown in Figure 20 provides a simple cross-reference between the problem areas discussed above and the methods discussed later.

READING REFERENCES

Most of the available textbooks on production management describe the principal areas of responsibility of production management, and provide a classification of the important problem areas. See, for example:

E. S. Buffa, *Modern Production Management*, 3rd. ed., Wiley, 1969.
R. Wild, *The Techniques of Production Management*, Holt, Rinehart & Winston, 1970.

CHAPTER 3

Mathematical Methods and Operational Research

In this and the following chapter we shall examine the use of mathematical methods in the design and operation of production systems. Adopting the somewhat loose definition of 'mathematical methods' developed in the previous chapter, we shall refer to methods derived from the fields of mathematics, statistics and economics. We shall not confine ourselves solely to optimizing methods, nor shall we be concerned solely, or even largely, with complex methods, but emphasis will be placed upon the mathematical or *analytical* aspects of the management of production. As far as possible we shall be concerned with the science of production management as opposed to the art. In fact we are concerned with a matter of emphasis, since the complexity of production management is such that the isolation of techniques, and the compartmentalization of approaches, is neither beneficial nor feasible.

For our purposes the origin of the methods discussed is unimportant – we shall be concerned only with relevance and usefulness. Many of the methods originated in, and were specifically developed for, the production function, whereas others were developed elsewhere and were subsequently used in production.

We propose to consider production management from an operational research (OR) or management science viewpoint. OR has been defined as 'the application of scientific methods, techniques and tools to problems involving the operation of a system so as to provide those in control of the system with optimal solutions to the problems'.* It is a science of recent origin; indeed the name was first used only thirty years ago. OR began to develop as a discipline in the United Kingdom during the second world war. During the war groups of scientists were formed

* C. W. Churchman, R. L. Ackoff, E. L. Arnoff, *Introduction to Operations Research*, Wiley, 1957.

by the Government to assist military personnel in finding solutions to strategic problems. These groups of scientists were multi-disciplinary and it soon became clear that such an approach to problem solving had immense benefits, for it was evident that the techniques and methods of one discipline were often relevant for studying problems in other areas. OR was thus born as an analytical and multi-disciplinary team approach to problem-solving. After the war OR was quickly adopted, first in industry and later in the public services, government, and education, such that at the present time the nature and purposes of OR are widely known.

The definition of OR given above is, in fact, slightly misleading because of the emphasis it places on the pursuit of optimal solutions. OR is by no means concerned solely with methods of optimizing; indeed recently there has been an upsurge of interest in the profession in non-optimizing methods. A large proportion of the well known 'mathematical' or 'analytical' management techniques were developed by OR workers, but equally, many of the subjects and methods of modern OR have been absorbed from other areas. For example, mathematical methods of stock control were first developed well in advance of the birth of OR, but since many such methods now comply with the general definition of OR they have been largely absorbed into that subject. OR, therefore, has since its comparatively recent birth grown in much the same way as any company might grow: by internal development and by a series of external acquisitions, a measure of vertical and horizontal integration has been achieved.*

The development of mathematical methods (using *our* definition of the term) for application in management is by no means the sole prerogative of OR workers since members of numerous other professions and disciplines, such as econometricians and engineers, are equally active. Nor would it be true to say that all OR has direct relevance in industry, yet as a body of knowledge

---

* This process of expansion and integration is by no means complete, indeed it might be considered that the most important change is still to be achieved, i.e. a merger of all bodies concerned with the improvement of operating efficiency.

and as a discipline, if not as a profession, OR is clearly of paramount importance to production management. Furthermore, OR is a useful vehicle for our examination of the mathematical or analytical aspects of production management. The definition of OR provides a conceptual base from which to work, and the 'problem forms' and techniques of OR provide us with methods of classification which will be of value to us later in this section.

OPERATIONAL RESEARCH PROBLEM FORMS*

We are unlikely to find two problems in production which are of an identical type, except in the case of extremely simple and/or abstract problems. Indeed one of the benefits of the OR discipline is that it inculcates a method of approach that does not rely upon the precise classification of problems, nor upon the application of a 'toolkit' of techniques. Nevertheless, although problems tend to differ in practice, this difference often derives from their content details rather than from their form. It will be of benefit at this stage to examine the form of problems, not only because solutions to problems derive firstly from an examination of their form, but also in order to examine the scope of OR. It is generally recognized that the following problem forms exist:

Allocation Problems

The problem of allocating or assigning resources or items occurs frequently in production, and also in other areas of business. Allocation problems – for example, the problem of allocating manufacturing facilities, allocating particular orders to specific machines, determining the production mix – occur whenever there are several methods of performing several tasks, and when facilities are not available in sufficient quantities to permit each

* The small book by Rivett and Ackoff (*A Manager's Guide to Operational Research*, Wiley, 1963) provides an excellent and simple description of OR problem forms. This section follows largely along these lines.

task to be done in the most efficient manner. Two principal types of allocation problem occur:

Problems involving the allocation of each task to one facility only

Problems involving the allocation of a set of tasks *together* to a set of facilities

The objective of allocation problems is, of course, related to cost and could be stated as follows – to allocate tasks to facilities in a manner which permits maximum efficiency or incurs least total cost.

Inventory Problems

The purposes of inventory have been discussed previously. Inventories, whether consisting of raw materials, components, indirect materials, finished goods, or semi-finished goods, represent idle resources. Clearly, therefore, the problem is how much inventory is required in order that the benefits from it can be obtained without undue waste of space, money or notional loss of interest on capital. The solution of such problems involves the balancing of counter-directional cost functions, that is costs which increase with increasing inventory, such as the cost of storage, insurance, obsolescence, and those which reduce with increasing inventory, such as the cost of possible stock-outs.

Simple inventory control theory is confined to situations which are assumed to be both static and deterministic, but in practice, the variables involved in such problems are frequently probabilistic, consequently a large amount of recent OR work has been devoted to this more complex type of problem.

Replacement Problems

Replacement problems occur frequently in industry and may involve items which deteriorate over a period of time following acquisition, such as machine tools, or items which are liable to sudden failure, such as light bulbs. Replacement problems lend themselves to various types of analysis varying from the highly complex statistical approach to simple simulations.

The optimum time for the replacement of deteriorating items is influenced by the nature of the increasing operating cost of such items, arising from the cost of increased maintenance, defective output, and the cost of replacement. The optimum time for replacement of items liable to sudden failure depends largely upon the costs associated with replacement and failure, and the probability of failure. The problems of replacement are, of course, closely associated with problems of maintenance since, for both types of item, repair maintenance may be appropriate, and preventive maintenance may be used either to reduce the probability of failure or to delay or retard deterioration.

Queueing (or Waiting-Line) Problems

A manufacturing company has been described as a very 'complex arrangement of queues'.

Figure 21 is a diagrammatic representation of a queueing situation, in which the problem is fairly complex, because of the

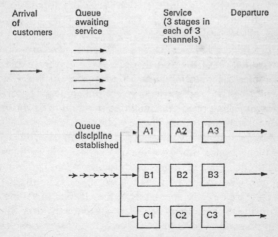

Figure 21 Representation of a Queueing Problem

existence of three service channels (*A*, *B* and *C*) each consisting of three stages (1, 2 and 3). This figure depicts a situation in which a queue of five customers await service. However, in practice the rate at which customers arrive at the service channels (the arrival rate) and/or the rate at which customers are served (the service rate) are likely to vary and consequently the queue length will also vary.

Queueing situations such as this are common in production where, to increase productivity, careful attention must be paid to the costs incurred. Whether in practice the manager's objective would be the minimization of average queue length, the minimization of service-station idle time, or the minimization of average queueing time, would depend upon the relative costs involved. However, whatever the objective the use of mathematical queueing theory may assist in the efficient design of such systems.

Sequencing and Routing Problems

In a queueing situation such as the one shown in Figure 21 customers may be serviced at the various stations in a particular order. In the case of a single station service facility, and also in the case of several sequential stations in which no passing is allowed, this order or sequence of customers is determined by the queue discipline. The sequencing problem, therefore, concerns the determination of the priority order of certain available items, for example, the determination of the order in which several items will be processed through several machines. The objective of such sequencing problems might be the minimum throughput time for all items, minimum facility idle time, etc.

Routing problems have a great deal in common with sequencing problems, since many production sequencing problems are essentially concerned with the determination of the order in which several processes shall be available to a certain job. In other words they are directly analogous to the classic 'travelling salesman' routing problem in which the objective is to determine the order in which an individual 'salesman' shall visit once each of several locations after leaving, and before returning to, base.

Search Problems

Search problems occur in very many situations, for example in mineral prospecting, auditing, strategic situations, problems of locational choice. It is rarely possible, because of limitations on resources (time, money), to conduct exhaustive searches, and so a problem arises as to the design of a search procedure which minimizes a combination of the cost of error and the actual cost of conducting the exercise.

Competitive or Bidding Problems

The mathematical treatment of competitive or bidding situations began over forty years ago.* Basically this OR problem form occurs whenever an individual's decision can be considered to be influenced by the decisions of other individuals, consequently this type of problem occurs widely and not only in industry.

Competitive situations may be classified as follows:†

Situations in which the competitor's action, or method of action, is known

Situations in which the action of competitors is not known but can be predicted, subject to certain probability of error

Situations in which nothing is known about the likely action of the competitor(s)

Gaming theory is a comparatively simple, but somewhat abstract, method of dealing with competitive situations from which statistical decision theory (a more practical approach) has developed.

OPERATIONAL RESEARCH TECHNIQUES

In the limited space available we cannot examine, even briefly, all the important OR techniques, and so we shall concentrate on the better-known ones.

* Early work was conducted by Von Neumann before 1930.
† After Rivett and Ackoff, op. cit., p. 51.

Mathematical Programming

Linear programming is one of the best-known OR techniques for solving certain types of allocation problems. As the name implies it is applicable only in situations which can be described by means of linear functions. For example, suppose a company makes two types of product, X and Y, each of which is an assembly of components A and B, as follows:

Product	Component (*no. required*)	
	A	B
X	2	2
Y	3	1

The maximum production for each product per week is 10 X and 10 Y.

If the company has a maximum of 40 of component A and 25 of component B available per week, it is clear that it will be unable to produce both the products at a maximum rate. The company is faced with a simple allocation problem: how many of X and Y to produce. Given the profit per product £5 per X and £7 per Y – this simple problem can easily be solved.

The objective is to maximize profit (P):

$$\text{max. } P = 5X + 7Y$$

It is, however, subjected to the following constraints:

Because of the limitation on A: $2X + 3Y \leqslant 40$
Because of the limitation on B: $2X + Y \leqslant 25$

If these linear functions are plotted as equations on a graph as shown in Figure 22, it is clear that if the objective is to determine values of X and Y which do not violate the above constraints, we are obliged to select a point within the shaded area on the graph. To maximize profit P we seek the largest total output of X and Y, and consequently the optimum allocation is given by one of the corners of the shaded area, in fact corner B:

No. of X produced = approx. 9
No. of Y produced = approx. 7
Profit = £94/wk.

54

If we could conveniently draw graphs in more than two dimensions, then by a similar procedure to the above, by examining the solution represented by the corners of the multi-dimen-

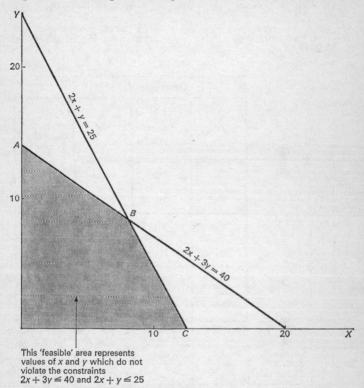

This 'feasible' area represents values of x and y which do not violate the constraints $2x + 3y \leqslant 40$ and $2x + y \leqslant 25$

Figure 22 Graphical Method of Solving Simple Linear Programming Problem

sional polygon, we could obtain an optimal solution to allocation problems involving several products. Fortunately an alternative mathematical procedure is available,* and consequently it is possible to devise a simple 'step-by-step' procedure† for finding

* The Gauss–Jordan complete elimination procedure.
† The 'Simplex' method of linear programming.

55

the optimal solution to more complex allocation problems of this type.

Allocation problems can also be represented by means of a matrix of the type shown in Figure 23. This figure represents a

The amount of resources allocated from source i_1 to destination j_1
(*Calculate*)

The cost associated with satisfying one unit of demand at j_1 from i_1
(*Given*)

		Destination			
		j_1	j_2	j_3	Total resources available at source
Source	i_1	a_{11} x_{11}	a_{12} x_{12}	a_{13} x_{13}	I_1
	i_2	a_{21} x_{21}	a_{22} x_{22}	a_{23} x_{23}	I_2
	i_3	a_{31} x_{31}	a_{32} x_{32}	a_{33} x_{33}	I_3
	Total resources required at each destination	J_1	J_2	J_3	$I_1 + I_2 + I_3$ $=$ $J_1 + J_2 + J_3$

Figure 23 Matrix Representation of an Allocation Problem

three-source, three-destination allocation problem; the resources together available at three sources must be used to satisfy the requirements of three destinations in such a way that the total cost of the allocation is minimized. The cost of allocating one unit of resource from each source to each destination (a_{ij}) is given. The optimum allocation (i.e. the x_{ij}'s) can be determined by means of a simple iterative procedure known as the *transportation method*.

The transportation problem is a special case of linear programming. Furthermore, there is a special case of the transportation problem known as the *assignment* problem which deals with the situation in which each source must be 'paired' with only one destination. This assignment problem can also be solved by an extremely simple algorithm.

If neither the constraints nor the objective, nor both, are of a linear form then we are faced with a *non-linear programming* problem. The solution of such problems is a good deal more complex than the simple type shown above; however, procedures are available, some of which depend upon introducing further variables to convert the functions to a linear form. Special procedures arc also available for the solution of linear programming problems in which certain variables must take on integer values.

Dynamic programming is a further type of mathematical programming used in non-static situations, for example in allocation problems involving a series of allocation decisions which are *not* independent.

Simulation and the Monte Carlo Method

Many management problems are too complicated to permit rigorous mathematical treatment, and consequently the only way in which the nature and complexities of such problems can be investigated is by experimentation. However, in the majority of cases, the OR worker or the production manager is unable to perform experiments on the actual business system since not only would this be a costly exercise but also the risk involved to the company would be intolerable. In such circumstances use must be made of representational models, which may be mechanical, analogue or digital. There are comparatively few business situations which lend themselves to mechanical simulation, and although analogue representation, particularly electrical analogues, is useful in certain circumstances, digital simulation is by far the most widely used representational technique.

Very often the reason why a particular problem or situation cannot be treated rigorously by mathematics or statistics is the fact that the variables involved do not conform to any of the defined statistical probability distributions, such as the Normal or Gaussian. In such cases the basis of a simulation approach is the use of random sampling from historical data; if past data is available, actual probability distributions can be drawn, and using random numbers, values can be selected from these distributions for use in the simulation exercise. This method of random sampling is known as the Monte Carlo method.

For example, if the cumulative probability distribution shown in Figure 24a describes the time interval between the successive arrival of cars at a toll booth, and if the cumulative distribution shown in Figure 24b represents the time cars must spend at the toll booth, then random sampling from both distributions will provide us with two sets of data which we can use to examine the toll booth situation. A simulation of activity at the toll booth over a very brief period of time is shown in Figure 24c, from which it can be seen that the toll booth spends a large portion of the time idle, but nevertheless two of the seven cars to arrive did have to wait for service. In practice a simulation exercise would be conducted over a considerably greater period than this, and use would probably be made of a digital computer.

Simulation is an invaluable and versatile OR technique which is widely used as a means of examining complex situations, to determine operating decisions, and as an aid to discover methods of improving the performance of such systems.

Queueing Theory

The toll booth situation described above is, of course, a queueing situation, and in fact simulation is an important technique in the solution of queueing problems. It is a comparatively simple queueing problem since it concerns only one service channel and one service station through which all customers must pass – rather like a single door into a department store. Had the arrival rate of the cars and the service rate at the booth conformed to

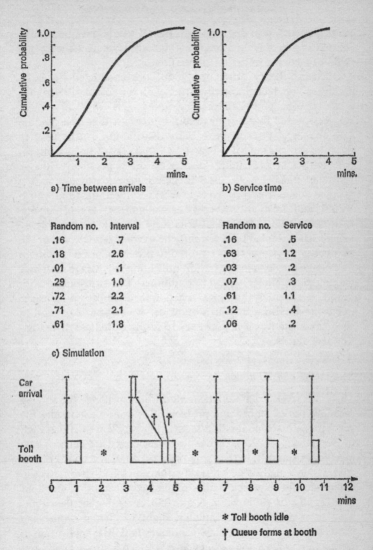

a) Time between arrivals

b) Service time

Random no.	Interval		Random no.	Service
.16	.7		.16	.5
.18	2.6		.63	1.2
.01	.1		.03	.2
.29	1.0		.07	.3
.72	2.2		.61	1.1
.71	2.1		.12	.4
.61	1.8		.06	.2

c) Simulation

Car arrival

Toll booth

* Toll booth idle
† Queue forms at booth

Figure 24

particular statistical distributions, then it would have been possible to examine this situation using statistical queueing theory and
without recourse to digital simulation.

Queueing theory originated with work conducted by A. K.
Erlang, a Dutch engineer concerned with the design of telephone
systems. Erlang noticed that incoming calls to telephone exchanges tended to occur at random intervals. If such a random
rate applies, a Poisson probability distribution can be used to
describe arrivals, and if it is assumed that service times conform
to a particular probability distribution it is possible to derive
formulae which can be used to determine such factors as the
average queue length or average service-station idle time, which
would result from given average arrival and service rates for one
or more service channels. Alternatively it would be possible by
using such formulae to determine the average service rate, or the
number of service stations required to provide a given maximum
or average queue, a given station utilization or average customer
waiting time, under specific conditions. The statistical theory
becomes extremely complex when one attempts to consider
queueing situations in which many service stations exist and in
such circumstances it is necessary to resort to the use of simulation techniques.

Sequencing and Routing

There are several mathematical algorithms available for solving
certain types of sequencing problem. For example, consider the
very simple machine loading/sequencing problem in which each
of five jobs (1, 2, 3, 4, 5) are to be processed on each of two
machines (A and B) in the same order; A first, B second (Figure
25a). Using a method developed by Johnson in 1954, we can easily
determine the sequence which minimizes the total throughput
time for all jobs, as shown in Figure 25b. Several other algorithms
have been developed for solving slightly different sequencing
problems, but in general such techniques find little application in
production where the sequencing problems are usually too
complex to permit rigorous treatment.

The best known routing problem is the travelling salesman problem for which several methods of solution have been developed. For example, the 'Branch and Bound' algorithm, although it has now found application in other areas, was

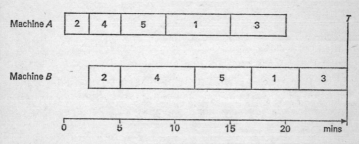

Job	Processing time on machine	
	A	B
1	6 mins	4 mins
2	2 "	3 "
3	5 "	2 "
4	3 "	7 "
5	4 "	5 "

Figure 25a

Figure 25b Optimum Sequence of Five Jobs, Assuming No Passing is Allowed, and Minimizing Throughout Time T

originally developed as a method of solving this type of problem. Basically the method involves the construction of a 'tree' representing all possible routes. For example, the tree shown in Figure 26 gives all possible routes for a 'three-stop' problem. Such trees are said to consist of nodes and branches (as shown). In practical cases it is not feasible to examine all possible routes, and consequently the concept of a 'bound' is used to facilitate solution. The 'lower bound', calculated for each node, gives the minimum duration of any path leaving that node. This lower bound figure facilitates solution since it enables us to concentrate on promising paths, those with low 'lower bounds', and provisionally to discard the others.

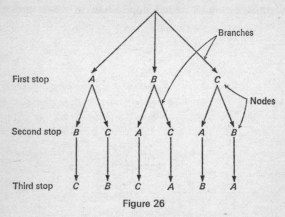

Figure 26

Game and Decision Theory

Game theory deals essentially with the first type of competitive situation described in the previous section: situations in which the competitor's action or method of action is known. The simplest

Player 2

		2_A	2_B	2_C
	1_A	2	−2	−1
Player 1	1_B	3	−5	1
	1_C	5	6	−10

Figure 27 'Pay-off' Matrix

form of competitive situation is the Two-Person, Zero-Sum game which may be conveniently represented by the 'pay-off' matrix shown in Figure 27. This figure represents a 3×3 game since each competitor or player has three strategies, *A*, *B* and *C*. The figures in the matrix represent the pay-offs to player 1 resulting from a pair of strategies; for example if player 1 chooses *B* and player 2 chooses *C*, player 1 gains one unit (the pay-off). If it is assumed that players behave rationally, then simple game theory may be used to 'solve' such a competitive problem, that is to determine the best strategy for the two players, and to determine the value of the game. Simple game theory can be extended to cover Zero-Sum games for an unlimited number of persons, but even so this type of problem rarely occurs in practice and hence game theory has found little practical use in industry. Nevertheless, although simple game theory is of limited practical value as an OR technique, it is of value as a means of conceptualizing competitive situations – for providing a framework within which such problems can be examined.

Statistical decision theory differs from game theory in that it admits the possibility that the actions of competitors may be neither deterministic nor rational. The simplest form of statistical decision theory deals with cases in which competitors' choice of strategies can be described by means of probabilities. In the more complex cases the action of competitors is *not* assumed to be rational, for example, competitive situations in which one player is 'nature' (e.g. the weather).

Operational Gaming is virtually a cross between game theory and simulation, and finds extensive use in the study of complex military and strategic situations. It is, in fact, a simulation exercise utilizing 'real' or human decision makers. This technique has, of course, been used for centuries as a military training method, particularly for officers, but more recently it has found quite widespread application in other spheres, for example in management education.

READING REFERENCES

Introduction to Operational Research:

Duckworth, E., *A Guide to Operational Research*, Methuen, 1962.
   Rivett, P., Ackoff, R. L., *A Manager's Guide to Operational Research*,
Wiley, 1963.

Introductory or Fundamental Operational Research Texts:

Ackoff, R. L., Sasieni, M. W., *Fundamentals of Operations Research*,
Wiley, 1968.

Operational Research in Production:

Special Edition, *The Production Engineer*, Institution of Production
Engineers, Vol. 46 No. 2, Feb. 1967.

Specific Operation Research Techniques:

Glicksman, A. M., *Linear Programming and the Theory of Games*,
Wiley, 1963.
   Hammersley, J. M., Handscomb, D. C., *Monte Carlo Methods*,
Methuen, 1964.
   Lee, A. M., *Applied Queueing Theory*, Macmillan, 1966.

CHAPTER 4

Mathematical Methods in the Design of Production Systems

WE have previously defined a complete production system as consisting essentially of the following:

The factory(ies) and the site(s)

The departments within the factory

The facilities within the departments, i.e. men, materials, and machines

A method of utilizing these facilities, i.e. a planning and controlling function

Clearly the purpose of such a system is the production of goods, and consequently a prerequisite for the design of a production system is the design of the product or products to be manufactured. In practice the design of the product(s) is rarely a major responsibility of production management, although ease of production is one important objective of product design.

Having determined the nature of the product, logically the next problem concerns the situation of the manufacturing facility – the plant location problem. The need to select a suitable geographical location for a new factory occurs infrequently, and it is a crucial, largely irreversible decision which has an important influence on the subsequent efficiency of the business.

PLANT LOCATION AND LAYOUT

Plant Location

Consider firstly the problem of locational choice facing the multi-factory company. A situation has arisen in which a company already operating one or more factories needs, because of expansion in production or changes in product range, to establish an additional factory. The problem is not merely the selection of an attractive location in some part of the country, but the decision as to which of numerous available locations will, when added to the existing locations, in some way maximize production efficiency or minimize operating costs.

If we consider this multi-plant locational choice problem as a distribution problem in which the objective is the minimization of total distribution costs, then an optimal solution can be obtained quite easily using the *transportation method of linear programming*. For example, if a company manufactures a particular product at two factories A and B for customers located at X, Y, and Z, the establishment of another factory (say at either C or D) will be necessary when the demands of X, Y, and Z exceed the combined production capacities of A and B. The problem facing the company, therefore, is whether to opt for situation (1), i.e. factories at A, B, and C, or situation (2), i.e. factories at A, B, and D.

Each of these situations can be represented by the transportation matrices shown in Figure 28. The figures in the 'cells' of the matrices are the costs associated with the transportation of one item from one factory to one customer, i.e. a_{AX}, a_{AY}, a_{AZ} are the costs of transporting one item from factory A to customers X, Y, and Z respectively. Given this information, together with the production capacities of each factory (x_A, x_B, and x_C), and the demand of each customer (x_X, x_Y, and x_Z), then the transportation method of linear programming can be used to determine the quantity of items to be dispatched from each factory to each customer in order to:

Satisfy total demand of each customer
Not exceed the production capacity of each factory
Minimize total distribution costs

The minimum total cost distribution arrangement for each alternative situation can thus be established, and the multi-plant location arrangement which minimizes total distribution costs can therefore be determined.

This same technique can be used to solve the location/distribution problem when the objective is maximization rather than minimization, for example the maximization of profit, where the figures in the cells of the transportation matrix represent the profits associated with the distribution of units from each factory to each customer. The transportation method is also applicable

		Customers			Production capacity of factory per year
		X	Y	Z	
Factories	A	a_{AX}	a_{AY}	a_{AZ}	x_A
	B	a_{BX}	a_{BY}	a_{BZ}	x_B
	C	a_{CX}	a_{CY}	a_{CZ}	x_C
Demand of customer per year		x_X	x_Y	x_Z	

		Customers			Production capacity of factory per year
		X	Y	Z	
Factories	A	a_{AX}	a_{AY}	a_{AZ}	x_A
	B	a_{BX}	a_{BY}	a_{BZ}	x_B
	D	a_{DX}	a_{DY}	a_{DZ}	x_D
Demand of customer per year		x_X	x_Y	x_Z	

Figure 28 Transportation Matrices for Factories at A, B and C and A, B and D

where total demand is not equal to total production capacity, the only modification necessary in such cases being the introduction of a 'dummy' row or column into the matrix to accommodate the excess demand or supply.

This method of linear programming is a mathematical optimizing technique appropriate for use in determining locations for multi-plant operations. Perhaps the principal disadvantage of the method is its inability to deal explicitly with more than a single criterion. Frequently management is unwilling or unable to specify a single criterion by which alternative locations will be evaluated. Often the choice of an additional location, or indeed a sole location in the case of a new business, is subject to several criteria, such as the following:

Proximity to markets (transportation)
Proximity to suppliers (transportation)
Cost of site
Cost of buildings
Rates

In such cases the transportation method is only of limited value.

If alternative locations are to be assessed strictly on a cost basis then a logical method of comparison would consist merely of summing the relevant cost for each alternative. However, certain criteria cannot easily be expressed in terms of costs (e.g. the pleasantness of a particular part of the country, the recreational facilities available). The attractiveness of each location in terms of these features may be expressed numerically using a rating scale in which 1 may represent most desirable and 10 least desirable, but we cannot merely add such figures to costs since they are completely different dimensions. A further complication arises when certain features or criteria are considered to be more important than others.

In circumstances such as these, use can be made of a technique known as *dimensional analysis* and the merit of a location can be evaluated as follows:

Merit of location $x = (F_1)^{W_1} \times (F_2)^{W_2} \times (F_3)^{W_3} \times \ldots (F_n)^{W_n}$
where $F_1 \ldots _n$ = factor such as a cost or rating
$W_1 \ldots _n$ = weighting attached to factor

High values reflect low merit.

For example, should we wish to choose one of two locations by

68

comparing them on a basis of five features, the optimal location (assuming accuracy of data) might be established as follows:

	Weight attached to feature	Location X	Location Y
Cost of land	2	10,000	7,000
Cost of buildings	2	20,000	21,000
Availability of labour*	3	5	8
Sports facilities*	1	6	2
Cost of transport	1	5,000	6,000

* Ranking score: 1 = Most attractive

10 = Least attractive

Value of $X = 10{,}000^2 \times 20{,}000^2 \times 5^3 \times 6 \times 5{,}000$

Value of $Y = 7{,}000^2 \times 21{,}000^2 \times 8^3 \times 2 \times 6{,}000$

$$\frac{\text{Value of } X}{\text{Value of } Y} = 1 \cdot 13$$

Location Y should therefore be selected.

These two mathematical methods are really quite different in both concept and application. The transportation method is a simple, rigorous, and useful method for obtaining an optimum solution for a rather specialized type of problem. Dimensional analysis, however, although less attractive mathematically, is an appropriate method for use in what might be considered more realistic situations. The transportation method is, in fact, a good example of a general mathematical algorithm, invaluable for solving a comparatively small range of rather specific problems, whereas dimensional analysis permits a more comprehensive consideration of similar problems, but for this reason the use of this method must inevitably lack some of the conclusiveness associated with the use of the linear programming algorithm.

PRODUCTION PLANNING

The problems of production planning undoubtedly provide considerable scope for the use of mathematical techniques, indeed such problems have engaged the attention of many mathematicians, statisticians, and operational research workers for some considerable time, and planning techniques such as network analysis are now widely adopted in industry.

For our purposes production planning will be defined as the determination, acquisition, and arrangement of all facilities necessary for future production of items. Consequently, production planning for a particular product is essentially a 'pre-production' activity, whereas the production control function derives from the implementation of these production plans, and is therefore largely a 'during production' activity.

Many of the particular problems of production planning depend upon the nature of the production system. For example, production planning in the mass production industry differs considerably from production planning in jobbing manufacture. There are, however, certain facets of production planning, such as sales forecasting, which are common to many situations and these can usefully be considered first.

Forecasting

A knowledge of expected demand for products is an essential pre-requisite for any planning of production. No one can see accurately into the future, and so the term optimal is meaningless in respect of forecasting. It is impossible to develop optimal forecasting methods since we can never be certain of the absolute accuracy of any forecast, or any forecasting procedure. Elsewhere in this chapter we have concentrated on those methods which ensure optimal results, but the same qualification cannot be applied for the purposes of selecting forecasting methods. We will therefore discuss a selection of mathematical, or rather statistical, techniques concentrating on those which are widely adopted in production.

In the simplest method of forecasting estimates of demand for a future period are based solely on actual demand during a previous period. This method has been used to construct forecast No. 1 in Figure 29. At the end of each period the expected sales for the following period have been determined by reference to actual sales for the present period, i.e. forecast sales for period $i + 1$ = Actual sales for period i.

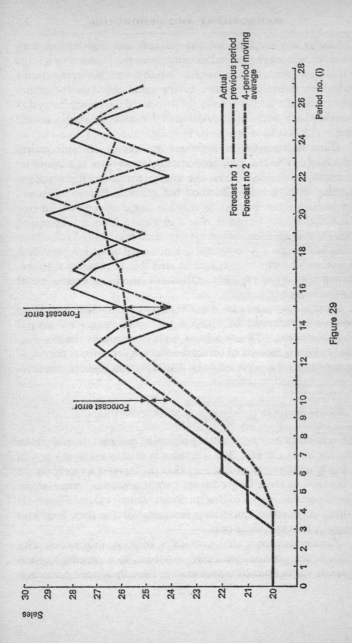

Figure 29

Clearly the accuracy of the forecast has deteriorated considerably during the period in which sales were subject to a large fluctuation. Because the forecast is based on one previous period's sales, the forecast fluctuates to the same extent as the actual figures, but the fluctuations in the forecasted figures are inevitably 'out of phase' with the fluctuation of the actual figures because of the one-period time-lag in the forecast.

Large fluctuations in forecasts are rarely desirable unless accuracy can be ensured, consequently some form of smoothing is usually advisable. The *moving average* method of forecasting is similar to the previous method but offers a degree of forecast smoothing since forecast figures are based on more than one historical figure. Forecast No. 2 in Figure 29 is a four-period moving average forecast for the data used previously, i.e. forecast sales for period $i + 1$ = average of actual sales for periods i, $i - 1$, $i - 2$ and $i - 3$. It can be seen that in this case the forecasted sales are not subject to the same amount of fluctuation as was previously the case.

Perhaps the principal disadvantage of the moving average method is the need to retain actual sales figures for several previous months. This disadvantage is overcome by the *exponential smoothing* method of forecasting which necessitates the retention of data for one period only. The exponential smoothing forecast is obtained as follows:

$$\text{Forecast} = \alpha \begin{pmatrix} \text{actual sales in} \\ \text{last period} \end{pmatrix} + (1 - \alpha) \begin{pmatrix} \text{forecasted sales} \\ \text{for last period} \end{pmatrix}$$

The choice of the exponential smoothing constant depends upon the nature of the data, but the value is usually about 0·1 or 0·2. Clearly small values of α ensure that the forecast is 'damped' or smoothed whereas larger values permit a greater 'response' of the forecasted value to the previous actual values. Figure 30 shows exponential smoothing forecasts for the data used previously, for two values of α.

The simple exponential smoothing forecast, in common with both of the previous methods, is subject to a time-lag; consequently where marked trends exist in the data a trend correction

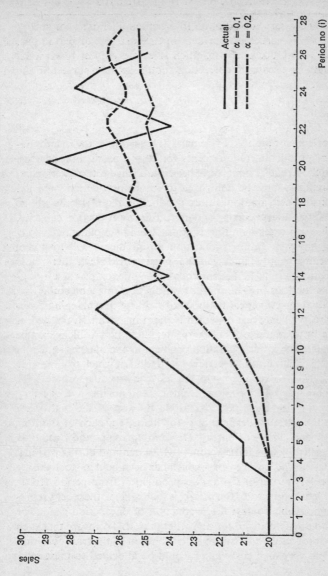

Figure 30 Forecast Using Exponential Smoothing

Actual
α = 0.1
α = 0.2

Period no (i)

Sales

will be necessary for accurate forecasting. The need for such a correction is particularly evident in the forecast for period nos. 3–4 in Figure 30. Likewise, when sales are subject to seasonal fluctuations a seasonal correction should be incorporated in the forecast figure.

Aggregate Planning

The principal objective of demand forecasting is the determination of production requirements for future production periods. When these requirements have been established future production requirements must be compared to future production capacity. In the simplest situation, future production requirements will be constant at a level corresponding to future production capacity, and in such cases planning is considerably simplified. In many cases, however, future production requirements will fluctuate, and consequently management must decide whether these fluctuations are to be accommodated by means of corresponding fluctuations in inventory, or production rates, or both.

Several mathematical methods of treating this planning problem are available, one of which is the transportation method of linear programming. The aggregate planning problem can be formulated as a transportation problem in the manner shown in Figure 31. This matrix describes a situation in which planning for four periods is required. On the left the various 'sources' for items are listed, i.e. opening inventory, and normal and overtime production for three periods. Along the top of the matrix are given the various 'destinations' for items, i.e. each of the four periods and closing inventory. Demand during period 1 can only be satisfied by opening inventory, whilst demand during period 2 can be satisfied by inventory (which has been held in stock during period 1 at a cost of C_1) and/or production from period 1. The lower left-hand part of the matrix is blank, since these cells represent impossible routes: the production of one period cannot be used to satisfy demand for an earlier period. To ensure that such cells or routes do not feature in the solution of the transportation problem very high cost values would be allocated to these cells.

Period no.		1	2	3	4	Closing inventory	Production capacity
Opening inventory		O	C_I	$2C_I$	$3C_I$	nC_I	I_0
1	Normal production	—	C_N	$C_N + C_I$	$C_N + 2C_I$	$C_N + nC_I$	N_1
1	Overtime production	—	C_O	$C_O + C_I$	$C_O + 2C_I$	$C_O + nC_I$	O_1
2	Normal production	—	—	C_N	$C_N + C_I$	$C_N + 2C_I$	N_2
2	Overtime production	—	—	C_O	$C_O + C_I$	$C_O + 2C_I$	O_2
3	Normal production	—	—	—	C_N	$C_N + nC_I$	N_3
3	Overtime production	—	—	—	C_O	$C_O + nC_I$	O_3
Demand		D_1	D_2	D_3	D_4	I_C	

Figure 31

where C_I = Inventory cost per item per period
C_N = Production cost per item in normal production
C_O = Production cost per item in overtime production
D = Demand
N, O = Production capacity

Other mathematical methods which have been used in aggregate planning include:

Linear programming using the simplex method.
The linear decision rule.*

Machine Assignment

The aggregate planning problem is concerned, in effect, with the problem of forward loading – the allocation of future demand to future facilities, or the provision of facilities to satisfy future demand. However, the solution of this planning problem does not eliminate the need for demand/facility allocation in the short term, e.g. the need to decide which of several available machines is to be used for processing a certain job.

Several mathematical methods of job/machine assignment are available but few, if any, are completely satisfactory in practice. For example, one simple technique is the index method which relies upon the calculation of an index number which is a measure of the benefit of using a particular machine to process a particular job. For example, if three machines (X, Y, Z) were available during a period in which a quantity of product A was to be manufactured, the index number for each machine could be calculated as follows:

	Processing time per product (hrs) for machine		
	X	Y	Z
Product A	20	15	17

$$\text{Index no. for machine } X = \frac{\begin{array}{c}\text{minimum processing}\\\text{time for product}\\\text{on any machine}\end{array} - \begin{array}{c}\text{processing time}\\\text{for product on}\\\text{this machine}\end{array}}{\begin{array}{c}\text{minimum processing time for product}\\\text{on any machine}\end{array}}$$

$$I_X = \frac{15 - 20}{15} = 0{\cdot}333$$

Similarly
$$I_Y = 0$$
$$I_Z = 0{\cdot}134$$

---

* Detailed description of these methods can be found in the references given at the end of the chapter.

Product	No. of items in order	Machine								
		X			Y			Z		
		Processing time per product (hrs)	Index no.	Time allocated to production of order	Processing time per product (hrs)	Index no.	Time allocated to production of order	Processing time per product (hrs)	Index no.	Time allocated to production of order
A	10	4·0	1·0		3·5	0·75		2·0	0	20
B	15	3·0	0·2		2·5	0	37·5	3·5	0·4	
C	45	2·0	0	90	4·0	1·0		4·5	1·25	
D	25	1·5	0		2·5	0·67	62·5	4·0	1·67	75
E	30	5·0	1·0		4·0	0·6		2·5	0	
Machine capacity (hrs)				100			100			150

Figure 32

If we adopt this criterion for the purposes of allocation product A should clearly be made on machine Y.

In a simple case such as this the calculation of index numbers was hardly necessary, but in cases involving a large number of machines *and* jobs, an index number *for each machine for each job* provides useful guidelines for job/machine allocation. For example, the allocation of jobs to machines shown in Figure 32, whilst not necessarily optimum, was facilitated by the calculation of index numbers.

Often, particularly in industries in which machinery is of an automatic or semi-automatic type, such as in the textile industry, an operator is required to attend to several machines. In such circumstances a different type of machine assignment problem is encountered, namely the man/machine assignment problem. The determination of the number of machines to allocate to one operator is an important production planning problem since the allocation of too few machines will result in idle time for the operator, and hence poor labour utilization and difficulties in establishing and operating incentive payment schemes, whilst the allocation of too many machines to the operator will result in machine idle time, and hence poor machine utilization. Figure 33a represents the first situation (too few machines), the second bar chart (b) represents the second situation (too many machines), whilst the third chart (c) represents the ideal situation in which neither man nor machines are idle. In a deterministic case such as this in which all machines have identical operating characteristics, the ideal number of machines to allocate to one operator can be obtained quite easily, either graphically as in Figure 34, or by use of the formula

$$N^1 = \frac{C + I_m}{C + I_o}$$

When the calculated value for N^1 is not an integer (a whole number), the decision whether to use the whole number greater than N^1 or the whole number less than N^1 will obviously be influenced by the relative cost of machine and operator idle time. In fact the ratio of the costs associated with each of these stra-

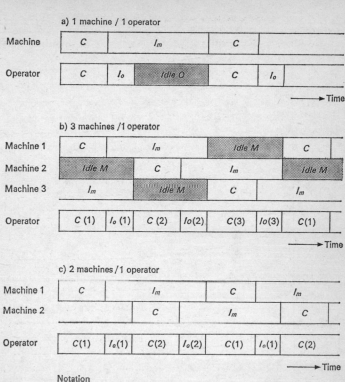

Notation

C Concurrent time operator and machine
I_m Independent machine operating time
I_o Independent operator operating time
Idle M Machine idle time
Idle O Operator idle time

Figure 33

tegies depends solely upon the ratio of the cost of operator and machine time, the number of machines allocated to the operator, and the ideal number of machines (N^1).[*] This relationship enables the curves shown in Figure 34 to be constructed. From these the optimum multi-machine/operator allocation can be determined.

[*] A derivation of this relationship can be found in S. Eilon, *Elements of Production Planning and Control*, Collier Macmillan, 1966.

79

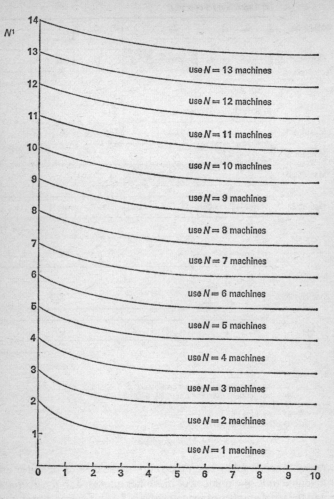

N^1

use $N = 13$ machines

use $N = 12$ machines

use $N = 11$ machines

use $N = 10$ machines

use $N = 9$ machines

use $N = 8$ machines

use $N = 7$ machines

use $N = 6$ machines

use $N = 5$ machines

use $N = 4$ machines

use $N = 3$ machines

use $N = 2$ machines

use $N = 1$ machines

$$\frac{\text{Cost associated with operator / unit time}}{\text{Cost associated with machine / unit time}}$$

Figure 34

Frequently the multi-machine assignment problem is considerably more complex than that described above. For example, the machine operating time (Im), or the concurrent operating time (C), may be variable, and then the determination of the optimum number of machines to assign to a single operator is particularly complex, and depends necessarily upon assumptions about the probability of machine stoppages, machine operating times, etc. Such a situation is in fact a complex queueing situation. For example, when an operator attends to several semi-automatic machines, if a machine stops or breaks down at a time when the operator is attending to one of the other machines, that machine must queue for the service of the operator. In such a situation *machine interference* is said to have occurred.

Numerous mathematical treatments of this multi-machine assignment or machine interference problem are available; however many of them, particularly those utilizing statistical queueing theory, are somewhat lengthy and complex, and therefore cannot be dealt with in detail here.

Project Planning – Network Analysis

Network analysis is one of numerous names used to describe what is perhaps the best known analytical planning technique. Other names include:

PERT (programme evaluation review technique)
CPA (critical path analysis)
CPN (critical path networks)

Network analysis has been widely used in industry and elsewhere as a planning technique, and particularly as a method for planning (and controlling) large complex projects of the type found in civil engineering, the aerospace industry, shipbuilding, etc.

In its simplest form planning by network analysis consists of the following steps:

Construct a network or arrow diagram to represent the project to be undertaken. Each individual job in the project is represented by an arrow or activity, and the arrangement of these activities in the diagram represents the order in which jobs will be done and the interdependence of jobs (see Figure 35);

Obtain an estimate of the duration of each activity in the network;

Using these activity durations, and with reference to the network logic, calculate the earliest and latest event dates, the earliest finish date for the project, and the amount of float or free time available for each activity (see Figure 35);

Compare the earliest finish date for the project with the required or scheduled finish date;

If the scheduled or required finish date is earlier than the calculated earliest finish date, attempt to reduce the duration of the project by rearrangement of activities and/or reduction in activity durations;

Use these activity durations and the calculated activity start dates in the production plan or schedule issued to the manufacturing departments.

Frequently in practice it is difficult to estimate with any accuracy the duration of jobs to be undertaken in a project; indeed the duration of such jobs may be influenced by unforeseen factors such as the weather, delays in the supply of materials. In other words, job or activity durations should perhaps be treated as variables rather than constants, and in such circumstances a slightly different computational procedure must be used to determine event dates and project durations. To facilitate network calculations it is usually assumed that the probability distribution for activity durations conforms to a beta distribution, and hence, given three time estimates for activities, the expected duration and the variance of the duration can be calculated for each activity as follows:

$$t_e = \frac{a + b + 4m}{6}$$

$$\sigma^2 = \frac{(b - a)^2}{36}$$

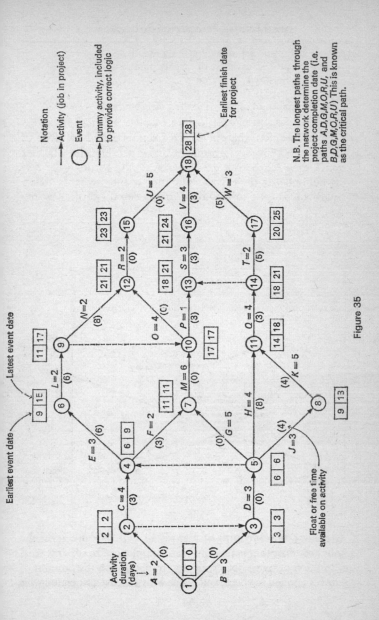

Figure 35

N.B. The longest paths through the network determine the project completion date (i.e. paths A,D,G,M,O,R,U, and B,D,G,M,O,R,U,) This is known as the critical path.

where a = optimistic estimate of activity duration
b = pessimistic estimate of activity duration
m = likely activity duration
t_e = expected activity duration
σ^2 = variance of activity duration distribution.

Certain other statistical assumptions enable calculations to be performed to determine the expected duration and variance of sequences of activities. Consequently, if we consider the sequence of activities which constitutes the critical path through the network, not only can the expected duration of the project be determined, but also the probability of completing the project by any given date.

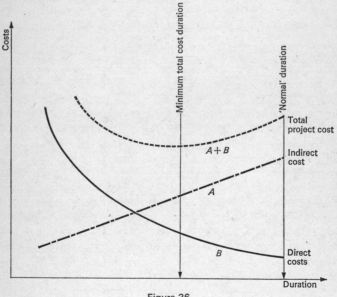

Figure 36

Of course the duration of many jobs will depend upon the amount of effort that is put into their completion. In other words, the duration of many jobs will vary inversely with the amount of resources applied to them, and hence with the cost associated with their completion. In such circumstances neither the minimum nor the maximum project duration is likely to be the same as the minimum cost project duration. Reductions in project duration are likely to lead to increases in the total direct costs associated with the use of resources, etc., and reductions in indirect costs such as administration, etc. Increases in project duration will have an opposite effect on these two cost categories. This situation is depicted in Figure 36, where increases in project duration result in increases in indirect costs (A), and reductions in direct costs (B).

A reduction in the duration of a project can be accomplished by reducing the duration of the critical paths, i.e. by spending more money (applying more resources) to one or more activities on the critical path.

Batch Production Planning

The dominant planning problem in batch production is undoubtedly that of determining production batch sizes, a problem which was first tackled mathematically by Harris in the early 1900s.[*]

Batch production is necessary when the production rate of facilities is in excess of the demand rate for the items produced. In other words, demand for the product is insufficient to permit the facilities to be utilized exclusively on its production. One solution, therefore, is to manufacture several products in batches on the same facilities. The size of these production batches clearly determines the number of occasions on which it is necessary to produce a product during a given period: increased batch size results in fewer production runs for that product and hence in fewer machine set-ups. However, increased batch size also results in increased average inventory levels, and hence an increase in the cost associated with storage. Clearly we are again faced with a counter-directional cost situation of the type depicted in Figure 36 where total cost is the sum of set-up costs (B) which reduce with increases in batch sizes, and inventory holding costs (A) which increase with increases in batch sizes.

[*] F. Harris, *Operations and Cost*, A. W. Shaw & Co., Chicago, 1915.

A batch production situation in which the entire manufactured batch becomes available to satisfy demand (e.g. is placed into finished stores) at the same time, is illustrated in Figure 37. In this case demand for, or usage of, the product is constant. The

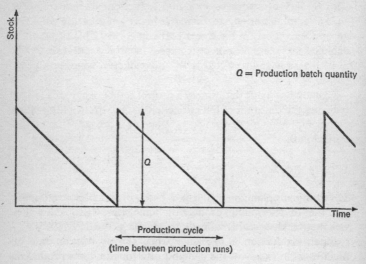

Figure 37

economic or optimum batch quantity Q^*, which minimizes the total costs of set-up and holding, can be determined from the following formula, or by use of the graph shown in Figure 38 which has been constructed using this same formula:

$$Q^* = \sqrt{\frac{2C_s r}{C_1}}$$

where C_s = machine set-up cost per batch
r = demand/unit of time
C_1 = holding or storage cost per item/per unit of time.

A slightly different situation arises when products are delivered into finished stock continuously during the production period – Figure 39. In this case the economic order quantity (Q^*), again

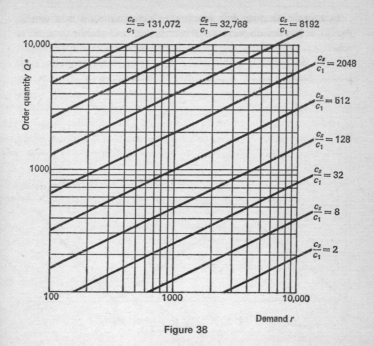

Figure 38

assuming demand or usage to be stable, can be found by use of the following formula:

$$Q^* = \sqrt{\frac{2C_s r}{C_1\left(1 - \frac{r}{p}\right)}}$$

where p = production rate, i.e. items/unit of time.

Because the total cost curve is comparatively flat at its lowest point, i.e. at the point corresponding to the economic batch quantity, it is possible in practice to adopt a policy of producing batches either somewhat greater than or less than the optimum number without incurring considerably increased costs. Indeed, in practice the optimum batch quantity is usually taken merely as one point in a range of acceptable batch sizes known as the production range.

87

Economic or optimum batch size determination is a simple matter if the assumption of deterministic and stable demand is made, i.e. the assumption that demand is constant at r items/unit of time, and that the value of r is known in advance. In such circumstances there is no necessity to maintain a buffer or safety

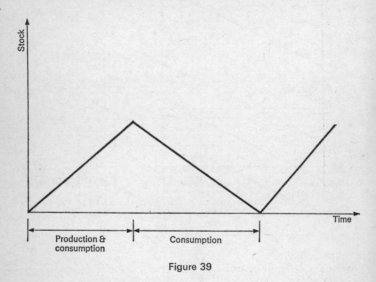

Figure 39

stock of items; only when demand is uncertain are buffer stocks necessary. Furthermore, in practice there is often a time lag between the beginning of the production of a batch of items and the time at which the first of those items are passed into stock (the production 'lead time'). The purpose of safety or buffer stock, therefore, is to protect against variations in demand and in the production lead time, or, if we put this slightly differently, the need for buffer stock arises from the occurrence of variations in lead time demand (Figure 40). The requisite buffer stock level depends upon the nature of the distribution of lead time demand (which can be determined by examination of historical production and demand data), and the service level required, i.e. the

88

maximum number of stockouts that are to be permitted during a given period.

The determination of production batch sizes and buffer stock levels for each product individually is rarely a sufficient solution

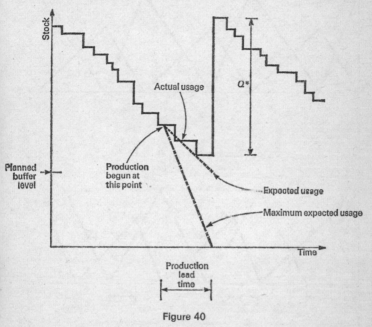

Figure 40

to the batch production planning problem. The number of batches to be produced in a given period, and hence the interval between production runs, can be determined as follows:

for the situation shown in Figure 37

time between production runs (production cycle) $= t = \dfrac{Q^*}{r} = \sqrt{\dfrac{2\overline{C_s}}{rC_1}}$

for the situation shown in Figure 39

$$\text{production cycle } t = \frac{Q^*}{r} = \frac{2C_s}{rC_1\left(1 - \dfrac{r}{p}\right)}$$

89

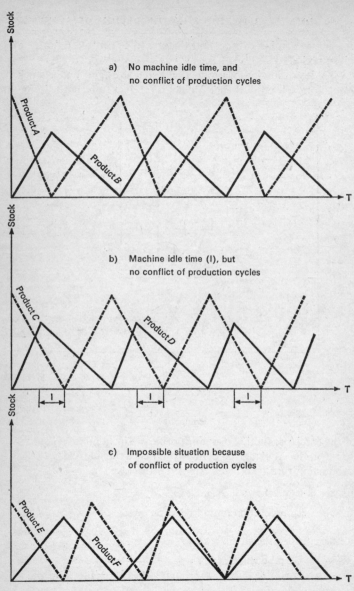

Figure 41 Batch Production, Two Products (production cycles determined individually)

However, in a situation in which two or more products are manufactured in batches on the same facilities, determination of batch sizes and production cycles for each product individually does not necessarily give rise to a feasible production schedule. For example, Figure 41 shows three possible results for a situation in which the production cycles for two products have been determined separately. The result shown in (a), in which no machine idle time or conflict between the products occurs, is an ideal situation which is unlikely to be achieved by considering products individually. The result shown in (b) is a practical situation since there is no conflict between products. There is, however, a certain amount of machine idle time which indicates that capacity is in excess of total demand. Result (c) is an impossible situation since the production schedule requires the simultaneous production of both products during certain periods.

		Succeeding model			
Cost of set-up	£	A	B	C	D
Preceding model	A	0	50	100	75
	B	60	0	50	75
	C	80	75	0	100
	D	90	70	65	0

Cost of one complete sequence = £270

Figure 42 Least Cost Assignment

To avoid the scheduling difficulties which are likely to arise from the 'individual' calculation of batch quantities, production cycles and batch sizes for products to be manufactured on the same facilities must be determined simultaneously. For example, for the situation shown in Figure 42, the total number of production cycles for each product (N) can be found by using the following formula:

$$N = \sqrt{\frac{\sum_{i=1}^{n} C_{1i} r_i \left(1 - \frac{r_i}{p_i}\right)}{2 \sum_{i=1}^{n} C_{si}}}$$

where C_{1i} = holding cost/unit time per product i $(i - 1,2,3 \ldots n)$
C_{si} = set-up cost for batch of product i
r_i = demand or usage rate for product i
p = production rate for product i

To use this formula the demand and production rates for each product must be expressed in the same units, e.g. in days of production. Having found the number of production cycles in this manner, the batch sizes can be found as follows:

$$\text{batch size} = Q_i = \frac{r_i}{N}$$

Mass Production Planning

Mathematical techniques are of comparatively little practical value for the design of assembly or flow lines; consequently important problems such as assembly line balancing are generally tackled by heuristic methods, and (increasingly) with the assistance of computer simulation. Numerous heuristic methods of balancing assembly lines are available and these will be dealt with in a later chapter.

It was pointed out in an earlier chapter that many assembly lines are designed to operate with a buffer stock of items between work stations. This buffer stock of items effectively decouples successive stations on the line, and consequently any slight delay at a station does not immediately affect the supply of work to subsequent stations on the assembly line. The determination of the optimum interstation buffer stock capacity (i.e. the maximum number of items permitted) can be considered as a statistical queueing problem. For example, making certain assumptions about the distribution of the processing times at the work stations, and the size of stocks before the first station on the line, the percentage utilization of a two station assembly line with various sized buffer stocks can be calculated. However, this statistical queueing theory approach is impractical for lines with many stations and consequently, in the past, research in this area has largely concentrated upon computer simulation methods.

Two problems for which mathematical techniques are of proven value both concern multi-model assembly lines, i.e. lines which are used for the manufacture of several products in entirely separate batches. The first problem concerns the determination of the batch sizes for each product, and the second the order in which the separate batches are to be manufactured. Batch size determination in this situation is a problem identical to that discussed earlier in this chapter, whereas the batch sequence problem is new to us at this stage, and merits further examination.

Cost of set-up £		Succeeding model			
		A	B	C	D
Preceding model	A	0	50	100	75
	B	60	0	50	75
	C	80	75	0	100
	D	90	70	65	0

Figure 43 Matrix Showing Set-up costs for Different Model Changes

The order in which batches of products should be made depends mainly upon the assembly line setting-up costs involved. The costs of changing the line set-up can be displayed as a matrix of the type shown in Figure 43, in which the figures in the cells represent the cost of changing the assembly line from an arrangement suitable for production of the preceding model to one suitable for production of the succeeding model. Having arranged the data in such a manner it may be possible to determine the sequence of models which minimizes total line setting-up costs, using the assignment method of linear programming. Notice that the zeros feature in the diagonal cells because no set-up costs are incurred unless a change of model occurs. To ensure that these cells do not feature in the assignment solution it is usual to attach high cost values to them. The least cost assignment for this particular example is indicated by the squares in the cells of the matrix shown in Figure 43. In other words, if we produce a batch of product A first the sequence thereafter should be B, D, C.

In this chapter we have discussed some (certainly not all, nor even the majority) of the mathematical methods which are of value in the design of production systems.

We can categorize such methods in several ways, for example optimizing/non-optimizing methods, mathematical/statistical methods, but perhaps the most useful classification for evaluation purposes is that of 'general' and 'specific' methods. Techniques such as linear programming and statistical queueing theory are general in that they have been developed as methods of solving problems of general importance such as the allocation or queueing problems. This type of problem is encountered frequently and not only in industry. For example, queueing problems occur in transport systems, at cash desks, toll booths, in telephone exchanges, as well as on assembly lines, and allocation problems are important not only in production planning but also in financial investment, aircraft flight scheduling, maintenance, etc. The very generality of these problems, however, must inevitably limit the value of the mathematical methods developed for their solution, if only because of the fact that such methods normally consider the optimisation of a single criterion, whereas in practice the number of criteria and the importance of any single criterion depend essentially upon the situation in which the problem occurs. It is for this reason that the general mathematical methods have proved to be of limited value in the design of production systems. They are not, of course, completely worthless since they often provide a means of obtaining a first solution, but few managers would be willing to base their decisions on this solution alone since it is in fact only a solution to a version – a simplified version – of the problem.

Network analysis and the numerous economic batch size formulae are good examples of the specific approach to problem solving in this area. Such methods are less open to criticism on grounds of inappropriateness, but can of course be criticized on grounds of insufficiency in the same manner as other methods.

As to the value of mathematical methods, it is clear that with the exception of economic batch size determination and network analysis few of the mathematical methods discussed have been shown to be indispensible and invaluable management tools; indeed it is perhaps true that even the limited practical value of many of the methods is evident only in respect of problems of secondary managerial importance. For example, in discussing the use of mathematical methods in production planning we were able to devote comparatively little space to the problems of scheduling and resource allocation.

Despite these criticisms there is little doubt that both the use of existing mathematical methods in production system design, and attempts to develop new methods, are completely justified. Present methods leave a great deal to be desired, it is true, but nevertheless the adoption of such methods is frequently justified in as much as they can be considered as offering signposts towards acceptable solutions. However, as always there is the danger that undisciplined and uneducated use of these methods will not only affect the overall efficiency of management decision making but may also jeopardize the future, perhaps more appropriate, application of mathematical methods.

READING REFERENCES

Most of the methods mentioned in this chapter are described in the following books:

Bowman, E. H., Fetter, R. B., *Analysis for Production and Operations Management*, Richard D. Irwin, 1967.

Eilon, S., *Elements of Production Planning and Control*, Collier-Macmillan, 1962.

Garrett, L. J., Silver, M., *Production Management Analysis*, Harcourt, Brace & World, 1966.

Magee, J. F., *Production Planning and Inventory Control*, McGraw-Hill, 1958.

Wild, R., *The Techniques of Production Management*, Holt, Rinehart & Winston, 1970.

The following are also of interest:

Silver, E. A., 'A Tutorial on Production Smoothing and Workforce Balancing', *Operations Research*, Nov./Dec. 1967. (This paper deals with aggregate planning.)

Young, H. H., 'Optimising Models for Production Lines', *Journal of Industrial Engineering*, V.XVIII, No. 1, 1967, pp. 70–78. (assembly line design).

CHAPTER 5

Mathematical Methods in the Operation of Production Systems

IN this chapter we shall deal with the operation of production systems. The previous chapter dealt largely with *planning* problems, and in this chapter we shall be concerned essentially with problems of *control*.

A good deal of confusion has arisen over the meaning of the term production control, since many writers use the term to cover both the planning and controlling functions. However, as was pointed out in an earlier chapter, the relative complexity and importance of the planning and control problems in production depend largely upon the nature of the product being manufactured and the type of manufacturing system. In many situations the problems of production control far outweigh those of production planning. A further source of confusion is the *scope* of production control. Many writers use the term broadly to include the control of both production and inventory. Such a definition is readily justified because of the necessary interrelation and interdependence of a company's production and inventory policies and practice. For example, future demand for a manufactured product can be satisfied either by existing stocks or by production, in the manner shown in Figure 44. In fact, as we have seen, one of the main purposes of inventory is to 'disconnect' production from demand and thus enable production policies to be adopted which result in a satisfactory utilization of facilities. To treat production/inventory systems explicitly in this compound way is beyond the scope of this book, and so in this chapter we discuss individual treatments of the topics in order to deal adequately with the use of mathematical techniques.

There is little confusion as to the meaning of the term quality control, except perhaps in the distinction between quality assurance and quality control. The former is concerned with

97

ensuring, normally by means of statistical sampling methods, that products or items inferior to specification are not accepted, whilst the latter, again depending upon statistical techniques, is concerned with avoiding the production of sub-specification items. Both of these topics will be dealt with briefly in this chapter.

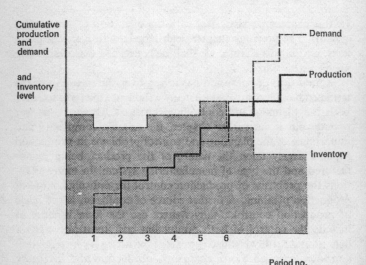

Figure 44 Batch Production – The Use of Inventory and Production to Satisfy Demand

Inventory control and quality control were the first aspects of production management for which satisfactory analytical treatments were developed, and since their initial development over forty years ago they have found widespread use in industry. In general, analytical methods find wider satisfactory application in the operation or control of production systems than in the design of such systems, and consequently there is perhaps more of practical value to discuss in this chapter.

STOCK OR INVENTORY CONTROL

The Order Quantity

Our discussion of mathematical methods of stock control will have a great deal in common with the previous discussion of batch production. Inventories may exist at many stages of the production process, e.g.:

In relation to the product $\begin{cases} \text{raw material and bought-in items} \\ \text{semi-finished goods} \\ \text{finished goods} \end{cases}$

Indirect items $\begin{cases} \text{tools, jigs, etc.} \\ \text{indirect materials} \\ \text{equipment} \end{cases}$

The production batch size clearly influences the inventory situation, therefore production batch size determination can be considered as an aspect of the in-process and finished goods stock control procedure. For the purpose of this discussion we shall refer to the purchased goods stock control policy, and hence our terminology is as follows:

Usage rate	r
Order quantity	Q
Price per item	p
Ordering cost/order	C_s
Stock holding cost/item/unit time	C_1

In the simplest case the economic or optimum size of the order quantity is influenced by two counter-directional costs: the total cost of holding stock, which increases with increased order quantities, and the total cost of ordering, which for a given period decreases with increased order quantities (Figure 45).

If we assume that all items in an order are delivered at the same time, and that the usage rate of these items is constant, then we can derive the following formula from which the economic order quantity (EOQ) can be calculated.

$$EOQ: Q^* = \sqrt{\frac{2C_s r}{C_1}}$$

(see p. 86)

99

In practice the price of purchased items is often subject to a quantity discount, the order of larger quantities from suppliers being rewarded by a reduction in unit prices. In such a case the determination of the economic order quantity by the above

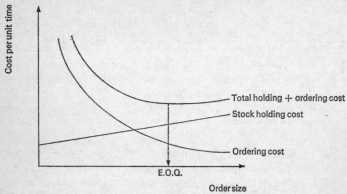

Figure 45 The Costs Influencing Order Size Determination

method is inadequate since the formula is derived only from a consideration of holding and ordering costs. Now we have a third cost which varies with order quantity, hence our order quantity must be determined by means of the model shown in Figure 46.

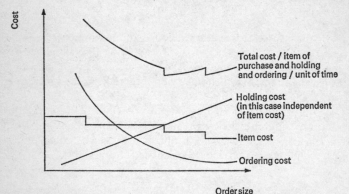

Figure 46 The Costs Influencing Order Size Determination

In this case the economic order quantity will occur at the lower end of one of the price ranges *or* at the lowest point of the continuous part of the curve, and may be determined as follows:

    (a) Calculate total cost for order quantity at lower end of each price range
    (b) Calculate Q^* using previous formula for each price range
    (c) Determine which of these Q^*s falls on total cost curve
    (d) Find total cost associated with this order quantity
    (e) Compare this cost with lowest determined from (a) to determine EOQ

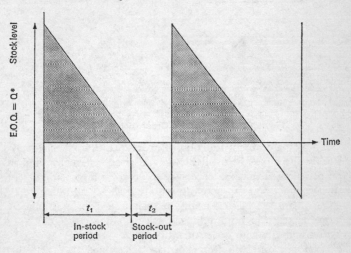

Figure 47 A Stock-out Inventory Policy

Occasionally a company may be prepared to tolerate stock-out – periods in which items are not available. Such a policy may be represented by Figure 47, and in such cases the EOQ can be determined from the following formula:

$$EOQ: Q^* = \sqrt{\frac{2C_s r}{C_1}} \sqrt{\frac{C_1 + C_2}{C_2}}$$

where C_2 = stock-out cost per item/unit time.

There are literally scores of economic order quantity formulae such as these, each of which has been developed to satisfy particular conditions. For example, in certain situations a proportion of the stock holding costs may vary with the order quantity. If, for example, holding cost is dependent upon the value of inventory, then it can be expressed as a percentage of item price, and furthermore, if quantity discounts are available

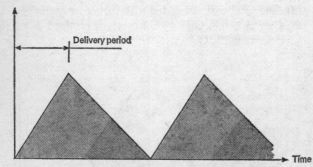

Figure 48 An Alternative Order (delivery model)

then holding cost is a function of order quantity. Alternatively, storage space may be available only in given increments, and so on occasions it may be necessary to accept a larger amount of storage space than is actually required. Thus the purchase of larger quantities of items may necessitate a disproportionately larger increase in holding cost, hence holding costs may vary discontinuously with order quantity.

Economic order quantities can be determined also for a different type of model (introduced in the previous chapter) in which delivery of items is continuous over a period. (Figure 48).

We must also consider the situation in which purchase orders cover more than one item. Our previous models have assumed ordering costs to be independent of order quantity, hence a logical extension would be the assumption that ordering costs are independent of both total order quantity and the number of items contained in that order. Consider the optimum ordering policies for each of the three items A, B, and C shown in Figure 49.

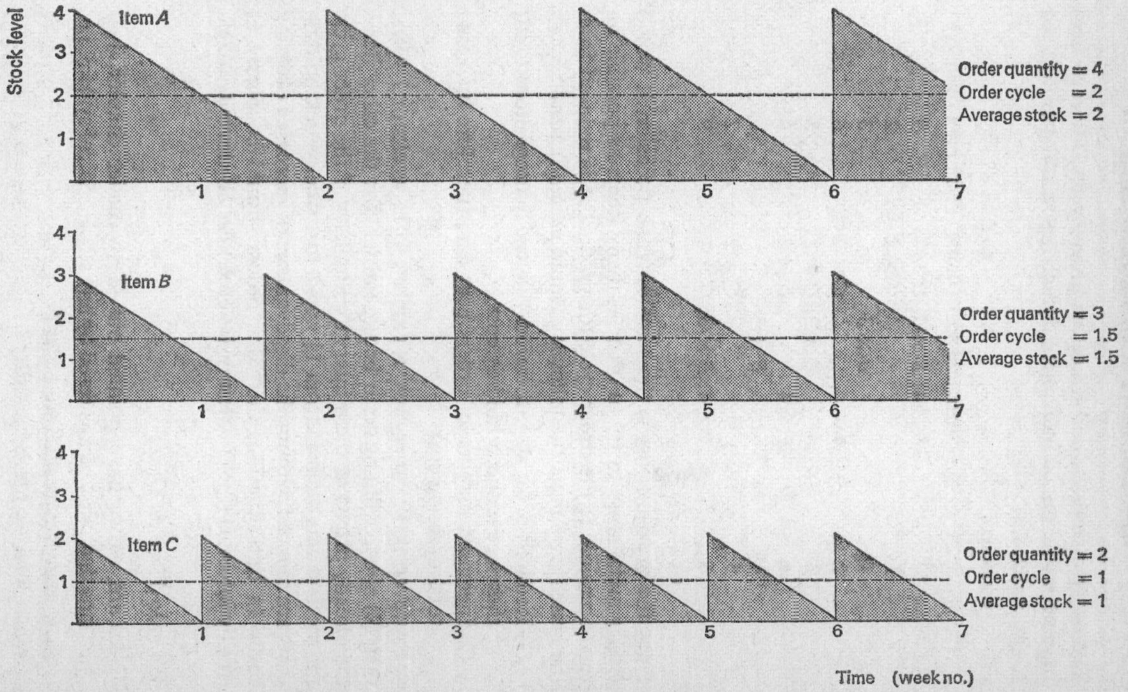

Item A

Order quantity	= 4
Order cycle	= 2
Average stock	= 2

Item B

Order quantity	= 3
Order cycle	= 1.5
Average stock	= 1.5

Item C

Order quantity	= 2
Order cycle	= 1
Average stock	= 1

Stock level

Time (week no.)

Figure 49

The order quantities, and hence the order cycles, for each item have been determined individually which has resulted in the need to order items as follows:

Week no.	Order	
	(Items and no. of units)	(Total no. of units)
0	$A \times 4$; $B \times 3$; $C \times 2$	9
1	$C \times 2$	2
$1\frac{1}{2}$	$B \times 3$	3
2	$A \times 4$ $C \times 2$	6
3	$B \times 3$; $C \times 2$	5
4	$A \times 4$ $C \times 2$	6
$4\frac{1}{2}$	$B \times 3$	3
5	$C \times 2$	2
6	$A \times 4$; $B \times 3$; $C \times 2$	9
etc.		

Since the ordering cost is the same on each occasion it would clearly make sense to try to order as many items as possible on each occasion. If the order cycle for product A is reduced from the present two units the following would *normally* result:

(1) Reduced order size; therefore reduced average stock level; therefore reduced holding cost

(2) Increased number of orders per year; therefore increased total ordering cost

However, if the order cycle is reduced to $1\frac{1}{2}$ weeks or 1 week, then (2) above will not occur because orders for the other items are already placed at these intervals. Similarly if the order cycle for product B is reduced from $1\frac{1}{2}$ weeks to 1 week stock holding costs are reduced without the disadvantage of increased ordering costs. In this situation, therefore, orders should be placed at weekly intervals (the smallest order cycle) for all three items.

When to Place an Order

There are, as we have pointed out in an earlier chapter, two questions that must be answered by any stock control system, i.e.

How many items shall we order?

When shall we place the order?

If demand is perfectly stable (as in Figures 47–9) and if order lead time is also known and constant, the second question is easily answered. However, if demand and/or order lead time is probabilistic, then the problem is not so easily solved. In such cases there is a need to utilize a buffer stock.

If the widely adopted 'order level' or 'two bin' system of stock control is used the answer to the following questions must be obtained:

What is the order quantity?
At what stock level must orders be placed?

If usage and/or order lead time are not constant a buffer stock must be used to protect against variations in usage during lead time (see Figure 40).

The choice of reorder level depends upon the variability of lead time usage and upon either the level of service required (the maximum number of stock-outs to be permitted during a given period), or the cost of stock-outs compared to the cost of holding stock. Given this information and providing usage is sufficiently stable to enable the EOQ formula to be used, the optimum reorder level can be calculated. For example, in Figure 50 the lead time usage probability distribution of an item (obtained from examination of records) is shown, and below it are shown three graphs which have been calculated to enable the necessary reorder level to be determined. In case (1) the expected number of stock-outs per year has been calculated, hence if a service level of 1 (i.e. a maximum number of one stock-out per year) is required, a reorder level of 38 or higher must be adopted. Similarly the other graphs enable a reorder level to be determined given the unit holding costs and the cost associated with stock-outs.

The problem of uncertainty of usage and lead time can of course be accommodated in the other main system of stock control, the order cycle system, in which orders for varying quantities are placed at constant intervals. Adopting this system in such circumstances normally results in higher average stock levels since the buffer level must be chosen to protect against

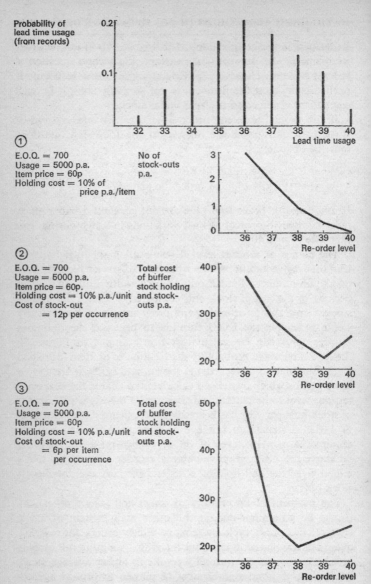

Probability of lead time usage (from records)

Lead time usage

① E.O.Q. = 700
Usage = 5000 p.a.
Item price = 60p
Holding cost = 10% of
price p.a./item

No of stock-outs p.a.

Re-order level

② E.O.Q. = 700
Usage = 5000 p.a.
Item price = 60p.
Holding cost = 10% p.a./unit
Cost of stock-out
= 12p per occurrence

Total cost of buffer stock holding and stock-outs p.a.

Re-order level

③ E.O.Q. = 700
Usage = 5000 p.a.
Item price = 60p
Holding cost = 10% p.a./unit
Cost of stock-out
= 6p per item
per occurrence

Total cost of buffer stock holding and stock-outs p.a.

Re-order level

Figure 50

variations in usage throughout the entire order cycle, whereas in the order level system buffer stock is required to protect against uncertainty during the lead time only.

In the previous discussion we have been concerned only with the deterministic and stable situation, that is the situation in which demand and delivery are known to be stable or sufficiently stable to permit the classical and simple economic order quantity treatments to be used. Buffer stocks are used to guard against uncertainty, and in many practical situations simple EOQ and reorder level or reorder cycle inventory control systems are perfectly adequate. However, since the purpose of this chapter is to review the use of mathematical methods, it is relevant to note at this juncture that numerous other mathematical and statistical procedures have been developed to deal with the problem of uncertainty in inventory systems.*

QUALITY ASSURANCE AND CONTROL

Quality Assurance and Acceptance Sampling

A company which is supplied with items some of which are defective not only stands to lose the purchase price of these items but also the subsequent cost of processing them. To avoid such a situation the company must take steps to assure itself that it takes delivery only of satisfactory items. Likewise the company's customers may also take steps to assure themselves that they accept only satisfactory products.

This quality assurance may be obtained in one or more ways, and at one or more times. Figure 51 represents some of the alternative procedures which might be adopted. Usually such steps to assure the quality of incoming or outgoing items consist essentially of a sampling procedure in which a proportion of a larger batch (say a delivery quantity) of items are subjected to quality inspection. This acceptance sampling procedure sometimes consists of merely inspecting a given percentage or number

* See, for example, the descriptions by S. Eilon in *Elements of Production Planning and Control*, Collier-Macmillan, 1962.

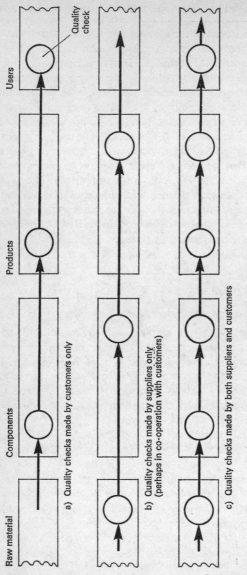

Raw material   Components   Products   Users

Quality check

a) Quality checks made by customers only

b) Quality checks made by suppliers only
(perhaps in co-operation with customers)

c) Quality checks made by both suppliers and customers

Figure 51

of all incoming or outgoing items, but in fact such a simple procedure is rarely entirely satisfactory since the inspection of a fixed proportion or number of items will often necessitate either an unduly large amount of work or result in inadequate protection. Clearly, if we are equipped with some knowledge of the reliability of the process by which the items have been produced, or if we have previous experience which indicates the likely percentage of defective items in a batch, then we are in a good position to determine the nature of the sampling process. Furthermore, only by hundred per cent inspection can we be certain that we have identified all defective items and consequently all sampling procedures are subject to risk – to the risk that the number of defectives found in a sample is not a true reflection of the number of defectives existing in the batch from which the sample was taken. Clearly the amount of risk that can be tolerated depends upon the nature of the items concerned and their purpose.

If, as is usual, items are classified as acceptable or not acceptable, then by making use of statistical probability theory it is possible to determine the probability of finding various numbers of defective items when taking a random sample from a batch containing a given proportion of defective items. Furthermore, it is then possible to construct a curve of the type shown in Figure 52, which shows the probability of finding fewer than a given number of defectives when inspecting samples of a certain size drawn from lots having a given proportion of defectives. Curves such as this are called operating characteristic (OC) curves. Such curves give the probability of accepting lots or batches of items having a given actual percentage defective (PD), when examined by means of a random sample size (n), and when the acceptable number of defectives in the sample is specified (C). An operating characteristics curve, therefore, indicates how well an acceptance sampling plan discriminates between 'good' and 'bad' lots. Notice that the larger the sample size the steeper the OC curve becomes, until ultimately, with hundred per cent or exhaustive sampling, the curve takes up a rectangular shape indicating that the plan is able to discriminate perfectly between 'good' and 'bad' lots (subject to human error during inspection).

If acceptance sampling is adopted for quality assurance purposes both the producer and the customer must accept a certain amount of risk. The consumer must accept a certain risk that lots

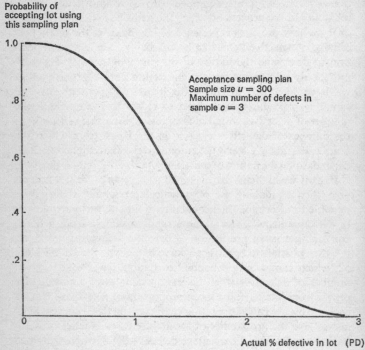

Figure 52 Operating Characteristic Curve

containing greater than the specified proportion of defectives are *accepted* by the sampling procedure, and the producer must accept a certain risk that lots containing less than the specified proportion of defectives are *rejected* by the sampling procedure. These two risks are known as the consumer's risk (β) and the producer's risk (α), and are associated with two quality levels known

respectively as the lot tolerance percent defective (LTPD) and
the acceptable quality level (AQL) (see Figure 53).

An acceptance sampling plan must be designed in such a way

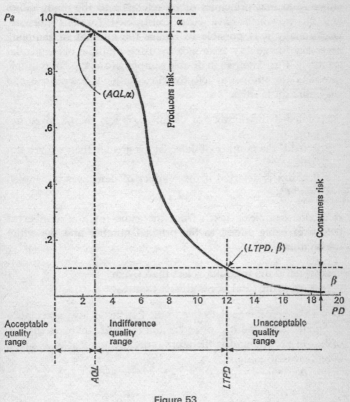

Figure 53

that there is a very high probability of accepting lots with better
than the AQL of defectives, and a very low probability of
accepting lots with worse than the LTPD level of defectives.
Indeed since any OC curve can be specified by only two points,
if these four values (α; AQL; β; LTPD) are given, then the two

points they represent can be used to specify the OC curve, and hence the acceptance sampling plan.

There are other types of acceptance sampling plan, all of which may be designed in a similar manner to that described above, and either from first principles or by reference to the many tables and charts which have been constructed for this purpose. Occasionally it is possible to reduce the amount of sampling necessary for quality assurance by using multiple or sequential sampling. For example, in double sampling (one type of multiple sampling) the number of defectives in a sample is determined, and the entire lot is either

accepted if the number of defectives is less than a given no. C_1, or

rejected if the number of defectives is greater than a given no. C_2, or

a decision is deferred if the number of defectives is between C_1 and C_2.

A second sample is taken from the same lot, the number of defectives being added to the original number and the entire lot is either

accepted if the total no. is less than C_2, or

rejected if the total no. is greater than C_2.

When the percentage defective in the batches is low, acceptance sampling using multiple or sequential methods involves the use of less inspection and is therefore more economical than single acceptance sampling.

Quality Control and Control Charts

The process by which defective items are rejected and satis-factory items accepted is of course only one part of the total process by which acceptable goods are provided by suppliers for customers. An equally important process is the one designed to prevent the production of defective items. Such a process is concerned with the control of in-process quality, and relies heavily upon the use of control charts.

Statistical quality control using control charts was first developed by Walter Shewhart in America in the early 1930s, and since then the principles and use of control charts have changed very little.

Variations in the dimensions of items produced by a piece of equipment occur because of either *chance* or *assignable* causes. Chance causes rarely result in large variations, and since they occur for many reasons and in a random manner their occurrence can be described by a statistical probability distribution. Assignable causes, such as differences or changes in materials or machines, or differences between operators, usually account for larger variations, and since such causes can be identified, their occurrence and effects can be controlled.

A control chart is used to define the limits of expected chance or random variations so that assignable variations can be identified and their causes determined and eliminated. For example, suppose we are concerned with an important dimension, say the length of a component. If we measure this dimension for all items produced during a given period, the mean or average and the standard deviation can be calculated. Now if we assume this dimension to be distributed according to the normal probability distribution, we can determine a larger and a smaller dimension beyond which we would not expect values to fall. In fact, if these two dimensions are placed 6 standard deviations apart, we would expect, on a basis of chance, only 0·27 per cent of the actual dimensions to fall beyond these limits. In other words, we can be reasonably certain that any observations falling beyond these limits do so because of assignable rather than chance reasons.

In practice two such sets of control limits are established:

Action Limits beyond which only 0·2 per cent of observations should fall and which act as a trigger for action to correct suspected faults in the production system.

113

Warning Limits beyond which only 5·0 per cent of observations should fall and which act a warning that service faults may be about to occur.

In practice it is tedious to calculate standard deviations, particularly in shop-floor conditions, and so in constructing control charts the *range* is often used as an approximation to the standard deviation. Furthermore, control charts are rarely constructed for individual values such as lengths, but are usually constructed for sample means. Not only is this a more convenient procedure, it is also statistically preferable since even in cases where the distri-

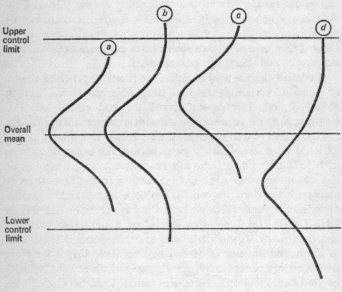

Upper control limit

Overall mean

Lower control limit

(a) Sampling distribution of means from which control limits were constructed

(b) Process out of control because of increase of process variability

(c) Process out of control because of change in process mean

(d) Process out of control because of increase of process variability and change in process mean

Figure 54

bution of individual observations does not conform to the normal distribution, the distribution of sample means may approximate quite closely to the normal.

A process may begin to produce defective items either because of a change in the mean value of a dimension and/or a change in the variability of that same dimension (see Figure 54). Consequently control charts for both sample means and variability are necessary to ensure the continuous production of acceptable items. For the reasons given above the standard deviation is rarely used as a measure of variability, and the use of control charts for sample means and ranges is virtually standard practice.

Figure 55 shows control charts for sample means and ranges. In this example the process is initially 'under control' (i.e. observations fall within the specified limits) but eventually control of the process is lost when sample means begin to fall firstly beyond the warning and secondly beyond the action limits. As control over the sample means is regained control of the process is lost because of increased variability.

Occasionally it may be impossible to determine the acceptability of items by means of measurement. For example, it may only be possible to examine the *attributes* of items in order to determine their acceptability, and so if process quality is to be monitored and maintained in such cases, control charts must be constructed on a somewhat different basis. Control of attributes may be achieved by the use of control charts for the fraction or proportion of defectives occurring in a batch. Such charts are constructed using the binomial probability distribution, and as before, limits are established at 3·09 and 1·96 standard deviations, using the formulae:

$$\text{warning limit} = \bar{p} \pm 1 \cdot 96 \sqrt{\frac{\bar{p}(1-\bar{p})}{n}}$$

$$\text{action limit} = \bar{p} \pm 3 \cdot 09 \sqrt{\frac{\bar{p}(1-\bar{p})}{n}}$$

where $\bar{p}$ is the proportion of defectives found from a pilot study
n is the sample size

115

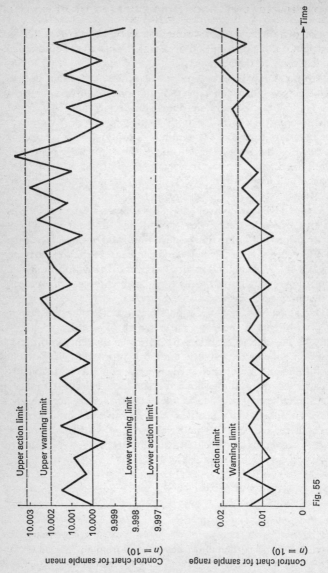

Figure 55 Simple Control Charts

Fig. 55

Figure 56 shows a 'proportion defective' or '*p*' chart. Notice that because the control limits are a function of the sample size the position of the limits must be recalculated whenever sample size changes.

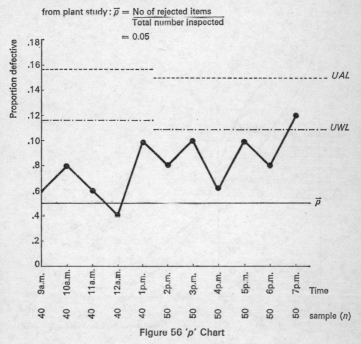

from plant study: $\bar{p} = \dfrac{\text{No of rejected items}}{\text{Total number inspected}}$

$= 0.05$

Figure 56 '*p*' Chart

MAINTENANCE AND REPLACEMENT OF FACILITIES

The objective of preventive maintenance is to reduce the need for breakdown maintenance, i.e. if applied effectively, increased preventive maintenance should result in a decrease in the number of machine breakdowns.

Preventive maintenance is of course costly, consequently we must apply such effort only where and when appropriate. Ideally, in fact. we would like to apply preventive maintenance to a piece of equipment just before that equipment would have otherwise broken down. However, since the operating life of equipment between breakdowns is rarely known with such accuracy, this is not often possible. We can, however, attempt to ensure from a

Percentage of breakdowns that
exceed a given operating cycle

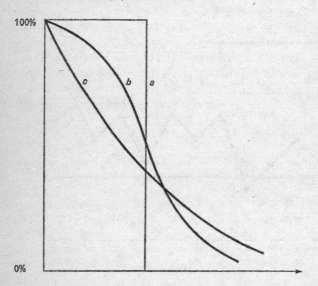

Operating life between breakdowns

a = Constant operating life
b = Reasonably constant operating life
c = Variable operating life
(approx. the exponential distribution)

Figure 57 Operating Life Curves

study of operating histories that equipment is suitable for preventive maintenance, i.e. that operating life between breakdowns is reasonably constant. It can be proved statistically that, in general, regular preventive maintenance will only maximize the operating efficiency of equipment when the operating life of the equipment between breakdowns has a variability less than that of the exponential distribution. In other words, referring to Figure 57, which shows various equipment operating life distributions, preventive maintenance is beneficial only when the operating life between breakdowns approaches the ideal situation represented by curve a. If the operating life of a piece of equipment can be represented by one of a family of low-variability statistical distributions, and if other factors such as the cost and average duration of both preventive maintenance and repair operations and the value of equipment output are known, then by using complex statistical queueing theory the optimal regular preventive maintenance schedule can be determined.

Strategy	Advantages	Disadvantages
(1) Replace each item when it fails	Ensures that no item in working order is ever disposed of. Ensures maximum utilization of every item	May involve a great deal of work since failure of items in any area may follow one another at close intervals
(2) Replace all items in a given area when one item in that area fails	May minimize amount of work involved since it is unlikely that after replacement further replacements in same area will be necessary immediately	Serviceable items are disposed of. Maximum utilization of each item is *not* ensured
(3) Replace all items that have been in service for longer than a given time in a given area when one item in that area fails	Advantage over (2) in that (a) only those serviceable items which are more likely to fail are replaced, and (b) greater utilization of items is likely	May involve more work than strategy (2)

Figure 58 Basic Strategies for the Replacement of Identical Items Each of Which is Subject to Possible Sudden Failure

Statistical queueing theory can also be used* in appropriate circumstances to schedule repair work, to determine the size and number of repair teams that should be available, to determine the optimum allocation of machines to teams, and to determine the average number of machines operating in such circumstances.

* See P. M. Morse, *Queues, Inventories and Maintenance*, Wiley, 1958.

Simulation is one operational research technique which is of considerable value in production management, and nowhere more so than in relation to replacement problems. Consider the problem facing a worker responsible for the replacement, when necessary, of numerous identical items each of which is likely to fail. For example, suppose a maintenance worker is responsible for the replacement of electrical bulbs in a building. The worker has three basic replacement strategies available to him, which are summarized in Figure 58.

The choice of strategy for a particular situation depends of course upon the operating life characteristics of the item, the

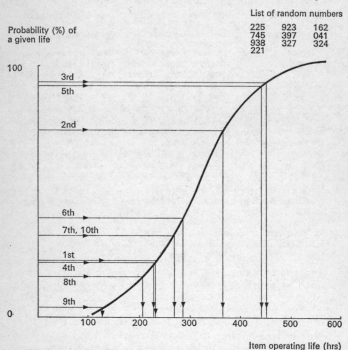

Figure 59 Cumulative Probability Distribution, from Which by Random Sampling the Life of 10 of Item No. 1 has been Obtained

number of items and their cost, and the cost of individual and group replacement. Simulation can be used to assist in the design of a replacement policy in the following manner:

(a) Use the Monte Carlo random sampling method to determine the operating life of each of a series of items, i.e.:

    (1) Determine the probability distribution for the operating life of the items concerned and draw the cumulative probability distribution for item operating life (see, for example, Figure 59).

    (2) Draw a list of random numbers between 0 and 100 from suitable random number tables.

    (3) Use these numbers in sampling from the cumulative probability distribution to establish the operating life of successive items (see Figure 59).

(b) Use this data to simulate the performance of the three strategies –

    (1) e.g. represent each strategy as a bar chart using the Monte Carlo data and indicating item replacements over a sufficiently long period (see Figure 60).

(c) Evaluate the merits of each replacement strategy, i.e.:

    (1) Determine the costs associated with replacement:
      (i) Cost of each item
      (ii) Cost of replacing one item at a time, two items together, three items together, etc.
      (iii) Cost associated with the failure of an item which is in service

    (2) For a given period and for each strategy determine the total cost involved.

PRODUCTION CONTROL

Production control in mass production is comparatively easy, mainly because of the inflexibility of this type of production system, because of the small range of items produced, and

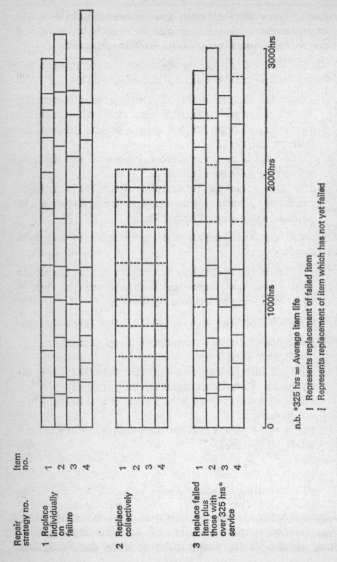

Figure 60 Graphical Simulation of Four Item Replacement Strategies

Based on a figure in R. Wild, *Techniques of Production Management*, Holt, Rinehart & Winston, 1970

because of the comparative accuracy of production planning. The principal purpose of control is to ensure the flow of material and items and few, if any, mathematical methods are needed or used for such a task.

In comparison, production control in jobbing production is an extremely difficult task because production planning in such circumstances cannot be performed with any degree of accuracy, because a large variety of (often new) items are involved, and because general-purpose manufacturing equipment is used. The principal purpose of control is to ensure that individual orders are delivered to customers no later than the time required. Traditionally production control in such situations relies heavily upon the efficiency and influence of the progress chaser, whose job is to ensure that items pass quickly from one operation to the next, that the manufacture of items is coordinated where necessary, that the necessary rectifications are made, and that management and the customer are kept informed of production progress. One important characteristic of jobbing production is the comparatively high work-in-progress which invariably exists, often alongside low machine utilization. Queues of jobs usually exist at each machine (unlike the assembly line), and consequently one important, perhaps the most important, function of jobbing production control is to determine the queue discipline, i.e. the order in which the awaiting jobs will be processed on the machine. In practice this *dispatching* decision is normally taken heuristically and will therefore be discussed in more detail in Chapter 6.

Production control in batch production is comparatively simple if batches are kept intact, i.e. successive operations on a batch of items are not begun until every item has completed the previous operation. In practice, however, batch splitting is often desirable since it not only permits a lower throughput time but also eases the work-in-progress stock problems (see Figure 61). One problem associated with batch splitting is the increased difficulty of production control. Since a single batch of items may be in process on several operations there is considerable difficulty in determining whether or not production is proceeding according

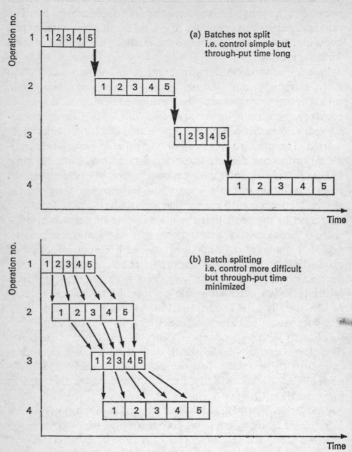

Figure 61 Processing a Batch of Five Items through Four Operations

to plan, i.e. whether or not at any time sufficient items have completed sufficient operations to enable a future delivery schedule to be met. The *line of balance* technique was developed with precisely this problem in mind. It is a useful and simple, though not yet widely adopted, method of both production planning and

124

controlling in batch production. The line of balance is in fact a line on a histogram showing the total number of items which should be completed at each operation by a given time in order that a given delivery schedule for the completed product can be satisfied. This line of balance is constructed from two pieces of information, namely the cumulative delivery schedule for the product (Figure 62), and the operations programme (Figure 63) which shows the order of all operations and the necessary lead time of intermediate operations over the final operation.

The line of balance can be constructed analytically or graphically from the information given in Figures 62 and 63. For example, since a cumulative delivery of 58 items is necessary by week 10, 58 items should have been completed at operation 10 by week 10. The cumulative completion of items at the previous operations can be calculated as follows:

Operation 9 has a lead time of two weeks over the final operation (op. 10), therefore at any time sufficient items must have been completed at op. 9 to fulfil the delivery schedule 2 weeks later. For example, at week 10 sufficient items must have completed op. 9 to satisfy delivery requirements for week 10–2–12. (This is sometimes called the equivalent week number.) Similar calculations can be performed to determine the required output at each of the previous operations (see Figure 64).

Control of production can be exercised by comparing actual progress at each operation at a given time with the requisite progress depicted by the line of balance (Figure 65); thus delays or shortages in production can be identified and perhaps corrected before delivery to the customer is affected.

Although we have devoted comparatively little of this chapter to a description of the use of the general mathematical techniques, it is again useful to distinguish between the two approaches – the use of general mathematical methods such as linear programming and queueing theory, and the use of specifically developed methods such as acceptance sampling, line of balance, batch size determination, etc. Linear programming can

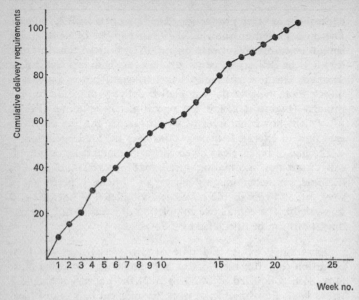

Figure 62 Cumulative Delivery Schedule for a Product

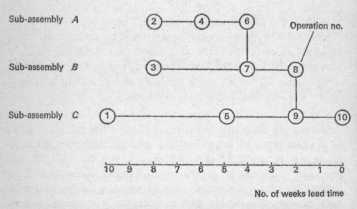

Figure 63 Operations Programme for a Product

be used in production control (particularly in sequencing) and in maintenance (particularly in determining the allocation of maintenance resources). Queueing theory is of course used extensively in the mathematical treatment of equipment maintenance policies, a subject which we have touched briefly upon in this chapter. It

Operation no.	Lead time over op. 10	Equivalent week no.	Cumulative no. of items to be completed at week 10 to satisfy delivery schedule
10	0	10	58
9	2	12	63
8	2	12	63
7	4	14	73
6	4	14	73
5	5	15	80
4	6	16	85
3	8	18	90
2	8	18	90
1	10	20	96

Figure 64 Calculation of Output Requirements at Each Op. for Week No. 10

is also possible to use statistical decision theory in maintenance decision-making. Dynamic programming, search theory, and analytical replacement theory are also relevant to the subject discussed in this chapter. It would, however, be true to say that, despite the obvious relevance of many such treatments, in practice their use in this area is minimal. One can argue of course that such a situation exists, not because of their lack of inherent usefulness, but because of the scepticism or ignorance of production managers. It is doubtless true that the majority of managers in this area are unfamiliar with the more recent and advanced developments in applied mathematics and statistics, indeed many are lamentably ignorant of even comparatively widely adopted analytical techniques, but this alone cannot be accepted as the reason for the non-application of certain analytical methods.

Over the last two decades, with the development of electronic computers as tools and operational research as a profession, there has been a considerable increase in the amount of research and development effort in the field of management science. There is of course inevitably a time-lag between development and application, but the fact nevertheless remains that comparatively little of this effort has yet influenced day-to-day business practice. Many would argue that the lack of application is an educational problem and therefore one which is likely to be largely overcome

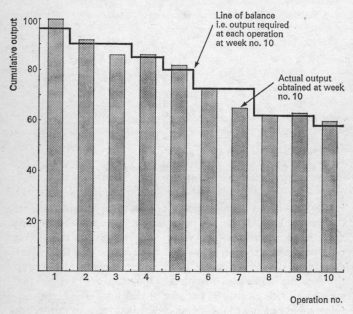

Figure 65 Line of Balance and Progress Chart for Week No. 10
(indicating tendency for operations on Sub-assembly B
to fall behind schedule)

in the near future thanks to the considerable growth of business education in this country. There is of course some truth in this but it is also regrettably true that much intellectual effort has been applied to theoretical, often esoteric, problems often only remotely associated with practical business problems.

Many people think that operational research workers, particularly those in academic institutions, devote insufficient of their efforts to the development of acceptable solutions to, or methods of treating, widespread practical problems, and too much of their efforts to the study of the abstract. For some considerable time it has been clear that many business problems, particularly those in the production function, are too complex to permit rigorous treatment. Equally it has been recognized that optimal solutions are not essential in many business situations, but that the need is for routine, reasonably simple and certainly comprehensive procedures for ensuring sufficiently *good* solutions. Fortunately there are signs that such facts are beginning to influence operational research workers, statisticians and systems analysts, who now increasingly recognize the need to devote more attention to fields such as heuristics and simulation. It is likely, then, that in the near future mathematical methods will have substantially more relevance in this field, and it is likely also that such methods will approximate more closely to the specific methods discussed previously, rather than to the general methods.

READING REFERENCES

Most of the topics discussed in this chapter are covered in the five books given as references for the previous chapter. The following books provide more details for three of the topics covered.

Hadley, Q., Whitin, T. M., *Analysis of Inventory Systems*, Prentice Hall, 1963.

Hopper, A. G., *Basic Statistical Quality Control*, McGraw-Hill, 1969.

Niland, P., *Production Planning Scheduling and Inventory Control*, Macmillan, 1970.

CHAPTER 6

Heuristic and Qualitative Methods

WERE it not for difficulties associated with structure and size, all business problems could be treated mathematically and optimal solutions obtained.

Clearly the first requirement for the successful application of mathematical optimizing techniques is an ability to express the problem in mathematical terms. Unless the nature of the problem is such that the variables involved can be expressed numerically, and unless mathematical expressions can be used to describe both the objectives and the constraints, then clearly rigorous mathematical analysis is impossible. Problems which do not conform with these requirements are said to be ill-structured, and so a well-structured problem is one which conforms to the following requirements:*

It can be described in terms of numerical variables, scalar and vector quantities

The goals to be attained can be specified in terms of a well-defined objective function – for example, the maximization of profit or the minimization of cost

There exist computational routines (algorithms) that permit the solution to be found and stated in actual numerical terms

Many problems, although well structured, cannot be solved by mathematical analysis because of the complexity, or more usually, because of the length of the calculations that would be involved. Consider for example, the apparently simple production-planning situation in which the problem is to determine the optimum sequence for each of five jobs through each of five machines. There are 5! (i.e $5 \times 4 \times 3 \times 2 \times 1 = 120$) different ways of putting the jobs on the first machine, 5! different ways of putting

* H. A. Simon, A. Newell, 'Heuristic Problem Solving: The Next Advance in Operations Research', *Operations Research*, V, 6, No. 1, 1958.

the jobs on the second machine etc., so there are $(5!)^5$, i.e. 24,883,200,000, different sequences for the five jobs on the five machines. Clearly to evaluate each of these separate solutions, even using a large computer, would be a formidable task. Although given sufficient time it would no doubt be possible to arrive at a mathematically derived optimum solution, the importance of the problem may not justify the time or cost involved in computation. Likewise, the mathematical solution of certain well-structured problems may require a method of analysis which, although perfectly feasible, is so complex as to be either unjustified by the importance of the problem or impractical because of the need for a rapid decision.

It is for reasons of structure and, more usually, of size that many problems facing management cannot be solved by the traditional techniques of operational research and statistics. Techniques such as linear programming and queueing theory are powerful analytical tools, but their application in business is severely limited. Such techniques are of course being developed and extended continuously, but even so it is unlikely that the traditional weapons of the operational research arsenal will ever be responsible solely or even largely for any substantial overall gain in managerial efficiency.

The practical ineffectualness of many of the existing and emerging mathematical optimizing techniques and the abstraction of a great deal of the work of operational research workers are facts which, thankfully, have been recognized by many people in that profession. As a result of this recognition, over the past ten years there has been a gradually accelerating movement towards the development and use of non-optimizing but adequate techniques appropriate for use in areas of managerial decision making hitherto unexplored by management science. Such techniques, commonly referred to as *heuristics*, have been derived and adopted from other areas of business, have been synthesized as the result of close observation of actual managerial action, and have been created on the basis of logic, experience, trial and error and experiment.

HEURISTIC METHODS

Until it was adopted by the management scientist the word 'heuristic' was normally used to describe a method of learning or an aid to discovery. Recently, however, the common meaning of the word has undergone a certain amount of change. Nowadays a heuristic may conveniently be defined as *any means, particularly a rule, principle or procedure intended to aid or facilitate problem-solving*. In other words, taken to its logical limit a heuristic is a rule of thumb. This last definition, whilst accurate, is perhaps unfortunate since it gives the impression of triviality. As we shall illustrate later such methods are often simple but rarely trivial.

The principal difference between heuristic methods and those discussed previously is that heuristic methods do not normally result in optimal solutions and are usually designed as a result of inductive rather than deductive reasoning. 'Inductive inference is the process of hypothesis-making in a trial-and-error fashion in order to draw conclusions or to solve problems. Whereas deductive inference is related to the mathematical methods currently in common use, *inductive inference* is related to the ingenuity and resourcefulness utilized in originally formulating such mathematical methods.'*

We all use methods and principles, which at a very basic level are heuristics. For example the fact that a red sky at night is often taken as an indication that the following day is likely to be clear and warm, is a heuristic, and perhaps not a very reliable method of weather forecasting. Other heuristics include:

production control – 'first come, first served', i.e. schedule first the first job to arrive

production planning – 'do the big jobs first'

investment – 'buy shares when prices begin to rise'

These are examples of one type of heuristic, i.e. simple rules. As indicated above a second, more complex and potentially more

* R. S. Ledley, *Programming and Utilizing Digital Computers*, McGraw-Hill, 1962.

important type of application concerns compound or sequential rules, normally referred to as *heuristic programmes*. In its simplest form a heuristic programme consists merely of a collection or set of heuristics arranged in such a way as to provide a procedure (often using a computer program) for solving a particular type of problem, subject to certain variations or complications. In more advanced form a heuristic programme is a type of inductive learning system based on a procedure capable of replacing heuristics with more efficient ones, and consequently capable of improving its problem-solving efficiency.

Heuristics are most widely used in management decision making to combat problems of size, because even with large high-speed computers it is rarely possible to conduct an exhaustive evaluation of all possible outcomes as a means of discovering the optimum solution. In such circumstances the initial problem is that of reducing the size of the problem before attempting a solution.

There are several available means of 'problem-shrinking,' not all of which may be relevant or possible in any particular situation. For example, it may be possible to identify classes of similar conditions or outcomes which can be grouped together to reduce the number of alternatives which it is necessary to evaluate. It may be possible to identify certain physical constraints which can be used to reduce the scope of the problem. Should either of these possibilities fail it will be necessary to search the available outcomes in pursuit of a near optimum. Such a search may be conducted on a random basis as in the case of Monte Carlo simulation (see Chapter 3), in which case the probability of finding an optimum solution improves with increases in the number of outcomes examined. As an alternative to this type of 'unintelligent' search it may be possible to devise a method of 'intelligent' search using heuristic procedures.

The difference between the three basic evaluational methods, i.e. complete evaluation, unintelligent search, and intelligent search, can be illustrated by means of the *decision tree* shown in Figure 66. In this diagram a circle represents a decision point and an arrow a particular decision. Two possible initial decisions are available, leading to decision points or *nodes* A1 or A2. Thereafter, two or three possible decisions respectively are available leading in turn to the final decision. These five decisions together give rise to fourteen possible outcomes. In such a simple situation an examination of each of these outcomes would

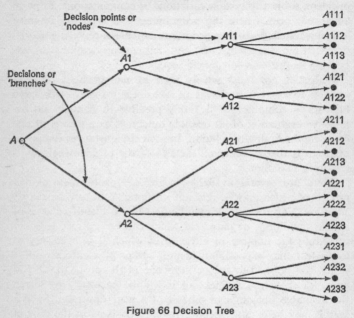

Figure 66 Decision Tree

not be unduly difficult, but in a more extensive case it may be necessary either to examine a random sample of the outcomes, using random number tables, or alternatively it may be possible to adopt a heuristic device in order to prune the 'dead wood' from the tree before evaluating a considerably smaller number of promising alternatives. Such a procedure might involve making a logical decision at each node and thus, by working through the tree, constructing one path to one outcome. There would, of course, be no guarantee that this outcome was optimal since a path which looks promising at early decision stages may deteriorate, and vice versa. Nevertheless, adequately designed heuristic procedures, providing they have been tested thoroughly and applied consistently, will usually yield acceptably good solutions in situations where more rigorous procedures are impractical.

THE USE OF HEURISTICS IN MANAGEMENT

It would be inaccurate to conclude that management is not a science solely because of the inadequacies of the available body of quantitative or mathematical knowledge, since in doing so one would be neglecting the importance of the behavioural sciences. Nevertheless, the inadequacy of the available quantitative knowledge does substantially affect the present state of both the theory and practice of management. Difficulties associated with problem structure and size are still the main hurdles obstructing efforts to achieve a greater utilization of mathematical and quantitative techniques in management, and the recent recognition of this fact, coupled with a greater mutual awareness between management and operational research workers, has undoubtedly sparked off considerable interest and development work in the field of heuristic methods. Whether one considers the area of heuristic methods to be associated primarily with operational research, or whether one considers it, like logic, judgement or intuition, to be a common possession, it is undoubtedly true that in the past such methods have played an essential and major part of managerial problem solving and decision making. The future is unlikely to see any change in this situation other than the wider recognition of the inevitable importance of heuristics and the consequent increase in efforts to add to, refine, and improve such methods.

HEURISTICS IN PRODUCTION MANAGEMENT

There is hardly an aspect of production management in which heuristic methods cannot or do not play an important part. Many of the heuristics currently in wide use in production management predate the general use of the word in this context, and consequently managers can perhaps be excused for feeling either irate or smug on seeing their methods and principles re-discovered.

In the later part of this chapter we shall discuss in more detail the use of both simple and complex heuristic methods in the design and operation of production systems, but as an indication of both the scope and importance of such methods we list below those areas of production management in which heurisics provide either the only feasible or the best methods of analysis:

Plant and facilities layout
Assembly line balancing
Production control and job sequencing
Resource allocation
Project planning
Problems of routing
Problems involving search

QUALITATIVE METHODS

A third type of decision making or problem solving procedure depends solely upon qualitative analysis. Both mathematical and heuristic methods have fundamental features in common since both normally involve a methodological routine, i.e. a set of defined steps or stages or a clearly defined set of rules or principles which if consistently and properly applied yield an optimum or near-optimum solution. In comparison qualitative decision-making depends predominantly upon individual judgement, experience and skill rather than the application of previously defined procedures. This does not mean that problems requiring qualitative decisions are necessarily of a non-recurring type, but rather that the nature of the problems is such that reliable routines are not available for their solution.

As an example consider the problems of method study, labour

selection, and product design. In each case there are available certain widely accepted procedures which in part assist in the solution of problems. In the case of method study, there are various means of recording existing work methods, using photographic techniques, process charts etc. and there are also available certain principles concerned with the efficiency of body movements. However, despite such procedures and principles, the design of efficient work methods is very largely a matter of judgement and experience. In designing a particular component or part, a draughtsman or engineer can, of course, make use of available formulae or even computer programs to determine stresses, fatigue life etc., but in the final analysis, it is his skill, experience and ability which largely determines the nature of the product. A manager responsible for staff selection can make use of psychometric tests to evaluate a candidate's personality and abilities, but in addition his decision will be influenced by his evaluation of the candidate's qualifications and experience, and his observations during a face to face interview.

Clearly the categorization of methods as qualitative or not, is a matter of emphasis. For the purposes of our discussion we have defined as qualitative those methods which are not contained in the other two previous categories, i.e. mathematical and heuristic.

THE USE OF QUALITATIVE METHODS IN MANAGEMENT

Generally speaking we can consider that what we have defined as qualitative methods constitute the art of management whereas the methods which form the other two categories constitute the science of management.

In this context art has been defined as 'a skill exercised in terms of the individual personality of the practitioner', and science as 'a unified and systematically arranged body of knowledge dealing with facts or truths and showing the operation of general laws or principles'.*

* L. A. Allen, *The Management Profession*, McGraw-Hill, 1964.

If we adopt these definitions there is no doubt that management is definitely an art and not yet a science. This is particularly evident when one considers what personal characteristics contribute to effective leadership or lead to effective decision-making.

QUALITATIVE METHODS IN PRODUCTION MANAGEMENT

A great deal of production management practice is qualitative or subjective in nature. This situation results from two obvious causes – the lack of more quantitative or objective procedures, and the reluctance or inability of those involved in production management to use the alternative methods presently available. This situation is typical of that existing in the whole sphere of management, and we can of course look forward to an inevitable but probably rather slow change in this state of affairs as efforts are made to improve managerial performance through both research and education.

Irrespective of any future growth in management education and research, and despite the impact of technological developments such as the computer and automation, a substantial proportion of practice in production management, both as regards the design and the operation of production systems, is likely to remain essentially qualitative.

The fact that a part of production management does not depend upon the sophisticated manipulation of figures, the machinations of computers or the intricacies of statistical inference should in no way detract from its importance. Without this feature of management there would be no need for managers, production managers included, to be equipped with those extensive characteristics such as insight, flexibility, patience and persuasiveness frequently listed by so many writers.

HEURISTIC AND QUALITATIVE METHODS
IN PRODUCTION MANAGEMENT

Two of the principal pioneers in the field of management were Frederick W. Taylor and Frank B. Gilbreth. These two American contemporaries were largely responsible, at the turn of the century, for developing what later became known as the *Scientific Management* movement. Both Taylor and Gilbreth were concerned with the nature and design of manual work. Taylor was concerned with, amongst many other things, work times, whilst Gilbreth, assisted by his wife, was concerned mainly with work methods. It was quickly recognized that these two ostensibly different approaches to the design of work were entirely complementary, and constituted the equally important parts of a field of study later known as *time and motion*, or *work study*.

Taylor enumerated several requirements of scientific management, three of which are as follows:

Investigate all aspects of work on a scientific basis, to establish the fundamental rules, laws, and formulae governing the best methods of working, and constituting a fair day's task.

Select, train, and develop each workman in accordance with the principles thus established.

Cooperate with the men by arranging conditions, services, guidance and methods of payment so that all the work is done, and is worth doing, according to the standards and principles developed.

The real importance of the scientific management movement is that it constituted the first attempt at a rational management theory, and although people such as Robert Owen and Charles Babbage had, some time before, advocated a similar approach to management and administration, Taylor, Gilbreth and their contemporaries were the first to adopt this so called 'scientific' approach. Nevertheless, by no stretch of the imagination can scientific management be considered as equivalent to management science, since although the approach of these early pioneers was rigorous, they were in fact dealing with matters about which it was, and still is, extremely difficult to formulate reliable rules or principles. From the point of view of production management, the main product of the scientific management movement is undoubtedly work study, and whilst much of work study practice is based on generally accepted principles, it remains substantially a non-mathematical, non-analytical technique.

WORK STUDY

Work study (see Figure 15) consists essentially of two parts, method study and work measurement.

Method Study

The objective of method study is the development of efficient work methods with respect to either existing jobs or proposed and new jobs. In the case of existing jobs there are seven steps involved, the first being the selection of jobs most suitable for study. In the case of new jobs, the problem of selection does not apply. These steps and their purpose in the case of both types of job are shown in Figure 67.

Work study is concerned principally with the elimination of inefficiencies in human manual work, and so at the *selection* stage it is important to ensure that manual work constitutes an important part of the job being considered.

Several methods of recording are available, the choice amongst which depends upon the amount of detail required. The better known recording methods are detailed in Figure 68, and three examples are given in Figures 69, 70 and 71.

Critical examination of the existing work method is an essential preliminary to any attempt to develop an improved method. There are several procedures available to assist in this examination but in essence this stage merely consists of asking the questions: what? where? when? how? why? who? Often this questioning procedure is broken down into two stages – *primary questions*

Method study step	Purpose: in the case of existing jobs	Purpose: in the case of new jobs
1 Select	Select jobs appropriate for study, i.e. jobs likely to produce significant savings as a result of study.	
2 Record	Make a record in sufficient detail of present work method together with all relevant information.	Using charts and diagrams etc. show in sufficient detail each of the alternative methods under consideration.
3 Examine	Study the record(s) critically with a view to improving method.	Study these alternatives critically with a view to selecting best or improving upon them.
4 Develop	Develop the most practical, economic and efficient work method available in given circumstances.	ditto ←
5 Define	Using charts, lists, etc. describe the method to be used in sufficient detail.	ditto ←
6 Install	Get the method adopted, re-train workers, provide equipment, test method, improve, etc.	ditto ←
7 Maintain	Ensure that the method is used in the manner intended. Check complaints and check improvements in productivity etc.	Ensure that the method is used in the manner intended. Check all complaints and measure productivity.

Figure 67

intended to establish the fundamental purpose or need for activities, and *secondary questions* whose purpose is to prompt the development of possible alternatives to the existing activities. Use is sometimes made of check lists or question sheets but of

141

Means of recording	System of recording	Type of record	Definition (where appropriate from BS 3138)	Amount of detail	Applications	Example
(1) Self			A record of a work method constructed by the worker himself	Usually very little e.g. often just a diary of activities or movements	To establish amount of time devoted to particular jobs etc.	
(2) Visual observation			Record depending upon memory of nature of work method obtained by means of actual visual observation	Usually little, although if applied selectively more detail can be both observed and 'digested'	As a preliminary investigation, to gain subjective impression to decide which type of detailed record to use	
(3) Paper and pencil	(a) Flow diagrams	(i) Flow diagram	A diagram or model, substantially to scale which shows the location of specific activities carried out and the routes followed by workers, materials or equipment in their execution	Shows location with respect to departments etc. and sequence of principal activities	Particularly useful as a means of studying layout	
		(ii) String diagram	A scale plan or model on which a thread is used to trace and measure the path of workers, materials or equipment during a specified sequence of events	Shows only extent and nature of movement between areas	Particularly useful as a means of studying layout	
		(iii) Travel chart	A tabular record for presenting quantitative data about the movement of workers,	Gives in quantitative terms extent of movement between areas	Particularly useful as a means of studying layout	

	over any given period of time			
(b) Multiple activity charts (activity analysis)	A chart on which the activities of more than one subject (worker, machine or equipment) are each recorded on a common time scale to show their inter-relationship	Difficult to record more than a limited n number of types of activity e.g. working, idle, delay etc.	As a preliminary investigation, or to study extent of occurrence of particular activities	Fig. 69
(c) Process charts				
(i) Outline	A process chart giving an overall picture by recording in sequence only the main operations and inspections	Shows principal elements only i.e. operations and inspections	As a preliminary investigation	Fig. 70
(ii) Flow process chart for man	A process chart setting out the flow of a product or a procedure by recording all events under review using the appropriate process chart symbols. This chart gives a record of all events associated with the operator	Operations, inspections, movements and delays associated with the worker	Normally used as the principal means of recording work methods	
(iii) Flow process chart for material	A process chart setting out the flow of a product or a procedure by recording all events under review using the appropriate process chart symbols. This chart gives a record of all events associated with the material	Operations, inspections, movements, delays and storage of material		

Figure 68 Method of Recording

Means of recording	System of recording	Type of record	Definition	Amount of detail	Applications	Example
		(iv) Flow process chart for man and material	A process chart setting out the sequence of the flow of a product or a procedure by recording all events under review using the appropriate process chart symbols. This chart gives a record of all events associated with man and materials	Operations, inspections, movements, delays and storage		
		(v) Flow process chart for equipment	A process chart setting out the sequence of the flow of a product or a procedure by recording all events under review using the appropriate process chart symbols. This chart shows how equipment is used	ditto		
		(vi) Two-handed (or operator)	A process chart in which the activities of a worker's hands (or limbs) are recorded in relationship to one another	Shows work method in same detail as above for each hand of operator at a given workplace	Operations at a workplace. To provide greater detail than other types of process chart	Fig. 71
	(d) SIMO (Simultaneous motion chart)		A chart, often based upon film analysis, used to record simultaneously on a common time scale the therbligs or groups of therbligs per-	Equivalent to above but gives much more detail i.e. in terms of 'work elements'	Where considerable detail is required, or as convenient record of film analysis	

			workers	
(4) Photography	(a) Memo-motion		A form of time lapse photography which records activity by a cine camera adapted to take pictures at longer intervals. The time intervals usually lie between $\frac{1}{2}$ sec. and 4 sec.	Little detail but compact activities occurring over a long period of time into shorter periods	For studying jobs with long cycle times, or jobs involving many people and movement over a large area
	(b) Movie film		The use of cine conventional photography to record methods of working either at a given workplace or over a larger area	Provides permanent record of actual activities in full detail	Permits a work method to be studied away from the job in a more convenient place and at a convenient time
	(c) Cyclegraphic	(i) Cyclegraph	A record of a path of movement, usually traced by a continuous source of light on a photograph preferably stereoscopic	Paths of movement of limbs within a fixed area	Movement of limbs at work place (infrequently used)
		(ii) Chronocyclegraph	A cyclegraph in which the light source is suitably interrupted so that the path appears as a series of pear-shaped spots, the pointed end indicating the direction of movement and the spacing indicating the speed of movement	Details of direction and speed of movement of limbs within a fixed area	Movement of limbs at a workplace with added time scale

Figure 68 Method of Recording—continued

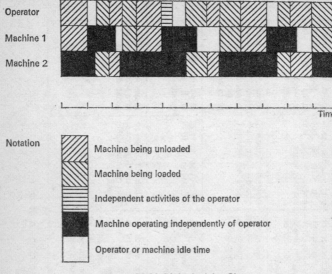

Operator	
Machine 1	
Machine 2	

Time

Notation

Machine being unloaded

Machine being loaded

Independent activities of the operator

Machine operating independently of operator

Operator or machine idle time

Figure 69 Multiple Activity Chart

course such devices are merely supportive and in no way serve as a substitute for the skills of the method study practitioner.

Similarly outline procedures are available to assist the method study practitioner in developing an improved work method. Three factors may contribute to improved work methods, namely:

Change in the work content or sequence
Change in the work environment
Change in workplace layout and design

A beneficial change in work content or sequence may be achieved through an examination of the following possibilities:

Attempt to eliminate activities
Attempt to combine two or more activities
Attempt to change the sequence of activities
Attempt to simplify activities

146

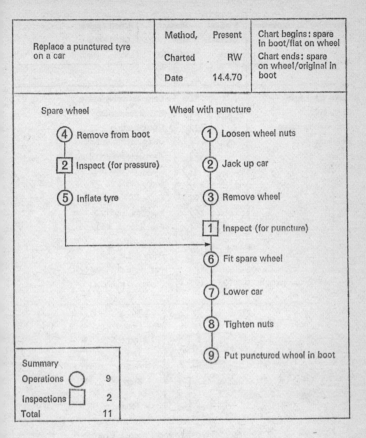

Replace a punctured tyre on a car	Method, Present	Chart begins: spare in boot/flat on wheel
	Charted RW	Chart ends: spare on wheel/original in boot
	Date 14.4.70	

Spare wheel   Wheel with puncture

④ Remove from boot   ① Loosen wheel nuts

☐2 Inspect (for pressure)   ② Jack up car

⑤ Inflate tyre   ③ Remove wheel

                            ☐1 Inspect (for puncture)

                            ⑥ Fit spare wheel

                            ⑦ Lower car

                            ⑧ Tighten nuts

                            ⑨ Put punctured wheel in boot

Summary
Operations ○   9
Inspections ☐   2
Total   11

Figure 70 Outline Process Chart

In attempting to develop improved work methods consideration must be given to *ergonomic* factors such as the nature of the work environment (heat, light, humidity etc.), the design of the tools and instruments used, and the layout and dimensions of the workplace. There has been a great deal of research in the field of ergonomics, and a large amount of data is available from many

147

Assembly of a pipe clip	Method Charted Date	Present RW 14·4·70	Chart begins Chart ends
	LH	RH	

	LH	RH	
Reach for U bolt	◁1	1▷	Carry assembly to bin
Grasp bolt	①	2▷	Reach for casting
Carry bolt to centre	◁2	①	Grasp casting
Hold bolt	②	3▷	Carry casting to bolt
		②	Assemble casting onto bolt
		4▷	Reach for first nut
		③	Grasp nut
		5▷	Carry nut to bolt
		④	Assemble nut onto bolt
		6▷	Reach for second nut
		⑤	Grasp nut
		7▷	Carry nut to bolt
		⑥	Assemble nut onto bolt
Release finished assembly to RH	③	⑦	Grasp assembly

Components	Layout	Summary		

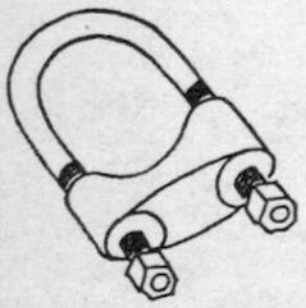

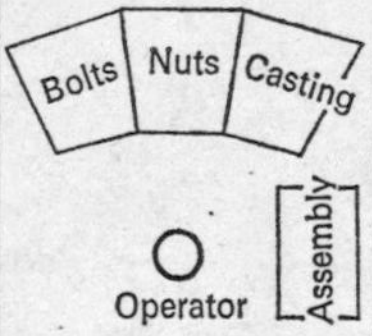

Bolts | Nuts | Casting

Operator   Assembly

Summary		LH	RH
Operations	○		
Inspections	■	3	7
Transports	▷	2	7
Delays	D		
Storage	▽		
Total		5	14

Figure 71 Two-handed Process Chart

texts and handbooks on the subject.* One of Frank and Lilian Gilbreth's notable achievements was their development of the principles of motion economy, consisting in effect of lists of guidelines or recommendations concerning the use of the worker's

* A series of booklets produced by the Ministry of Technology entitled 'Ergonomics in Industry' provide a very useful introduction to the subject (see References).

body, the design of the workplace, and the design of equipment. Some of these principles are listed in Figure 72.

(1) It is easier and more natural to work with two hands rather than one
(2) The two hands should begin and complete their movements at the same time
(3) The motion of the arms should be in opposite directions and should be made simultaneously and symmetrically
(4) Hands and arms naturally move smoothly in arcs, and this is preferable to straight-line movement
(5) Hand, arm, and body movements should be confined to the lowest classification with which it is possible satisfactorily to perform the work
    e.g. Gilbreth's classification of hand movements:
    (i) Fingers
    (ii) Fingers and wrists
    (iii) Fingers, wrists and forearm
    (iv) Fingers, wrists, forearm and upper arm
    (v) Fingers, wrists, forearm, upper arm and shoulder
(6) Work should be arranged to permit natural and habitual movements
(7) Movements should be continuous and smooth with no sharp changes in direction or speed
(8) The two hands should not, except during rest periods be idle at the same time
(9) Whenever possible momentum should be employed to assist the work, and minimized if it must be overcome by the worker
(10) Ballistic movements are faster, easier and more accurate than controlled (fixation) movements
(11) The need to fix and focus the eyes on an object should be minimized, and when this is necessary, the occasions should occur as close together as possible

Figure 72 Principles of Motion Economy (use of the worker's body)

Reprinted by permission from R. Wild, *The Techniques of Production Management*, Holt, Rinehart & Winston, 1970.

Work Measurement

Irrespective of the limitations of the techniques available, and despite its occasional unpopularity in practice, work measurement is an essential feature of production management. The measurement of work to obtain standard times for jobs is necessary for the implementation of most types of incentive payment systems, for accurate production planning and to provide data by means of which alternative work methods can be objectively compared.

Work measurement is defined as 'the application of techniques designed to establish the time for a qualified worker to carry out a specified job at a defined level of performance' (BS 3138). Basically there are two means by which such times can be established:

By studying a worker performing the job in question (i.e. direct work measurement)

By constructing or otherwise obtaining a time without the need to see the job performed (i.e. indirect work measurement)

Within each of these categories there are several techniques or methods available. The better-known methods and their uses are described in Figure 73.

The traditional and still the most popular method of work measurement is *time study* which involves the following steps:

(1) Get all *details* of the job to be measured. It is necessary to record details of the work place, work conditions, etc. which apply at the time of the study, in order to prevent the same data being used in the future in entirely different circumstances.

(2) Divide the job into elements. Because it is difficult to obtain an accurate time for the complete job by direct timing, it is necessary to divide the job into smaller units or elements. The nature and the size of these elements will be determined purely for reasons of convenience. Elements must not be too short for timing by hand-operated stop watch, nor should they be too long. The elements should, if possible, have a clearly defined starting and finishing point to assist during timing. Elements which occur regularly with every repeat of the job cycle should be separated from those that occur only intermittently, and elements concerned with the operator should be separated from those concerned with the machine. Often data obtained during time study exercises are collected and retained and used at a later date in constructing or synthesizing times for jobs. If the data is to be used for this purpose, it is obviously important that elements should be both logically and clearly defined.

(3) Elemental times obtained by an observer using a stop watch are, of course, actual times, and are not necessarily the times that should be required by an operator working at a defined level of performance. It is necessary, therefore, whilst timing the operator, to make an assessment of the rate of working, in other words the observer must assess the difference between the actual observed rate and a previously defined norm. To assist him to *rate* operators in this manner, the time-study practitioner will have been trained, usually by means of cine films, to recognize the rate of work corresponding to *standard performance*. This standard performance is defined as 'the rate of output which *qualified* workers will naturally achieve without over-exertion as an average over the working day or shift provided they know and adhere to the specified method and provided they are motivated to apply themselves to their work' (BS 3138). Using British Standards notation, standard performance is considered to be equal to 100, and so rates of 50 and 200 correspond to half and twice the standard rate of working.

(4) Decide *how many times must be obtained for each element*. The number of observations of each element will be determined by the amount of accuracy required, the 'confidence level' required, and the variability of the element times. Often a 95% confidence level and $\pm 5\%$ accuracy are specified (i.e. chances must be at least 95 out of every 100 that the average time obtained during the study will be in error by no more than plus or minus 5%).

The number of work cycles to time can be calculated from formulae such as the following:

$$N^1 = \left(\frac{40\sqrt{N\Sigma X^2 - (\Sigma X)^2}}{\Sigma X} \right)$$

where N^1 = number of times to obtain for each element to give 95 per cent confidence level and +5 per cent accuracy
where N and X are obtained during either a pilot investigation or during the first part of the actual time study investigation
$\quad N$ = number of times obtained
$\quad X$ = each element time
$\quad \Sigma X$ = sum of N element times

151

	Technique	Definition (BS 3138)	Steps involved	Accuracy/Detail	Applications

Direct work measurement	(1) Activity sampling	A technique in which a large number of instantaneous observations are made over a period of time of a group of machines, processes or workers. Each observation records what is happening at that instant and the percentage of observations recorded for a particular activity or delay is a measure of the percentage of time during which that activity or delay occurs	(1) Get all details of job(s) to be measured
			(2) Divide job into activities
			(3) Conduct pilot study to:
			  (a) determine number of observations
			  (b) check method
			(4) Conduct study, make readings
			(5) Calculate proportion of time for each activity
				Gives information concerning proportion of time spent on each activity only	Intermittent work. Long cycle times. As a preliminary investigation

	(2) Time study	A work measurement technique for recording the times and rates of working for the elements of a specified job carried out under specified conditions, and for analysing the data so as to obtain the time necessary for carrying out the job at a defined level of performance	(1) Get all information concerning job to be measured (2) Divide job into *elements* (3) Time and rate the elements (4) Determine number of cycles to time (5) Determine allowances (6) Calculate standard time for job	Amount of detail is determined by Step 2 and accuracy is determined largely by the process of *rating* (Step 3) which is largest subjective area of Time Study	Widely used particularly for direct work. May be used as a preliminary to generating synthetic data
Indirect work measurement	(1) Synthesis	A work measurement technique for building up the time for a job at a defined level of performance by totalling ele...	(1) Get all details of job to be measured (2) Divide job into elements (3) Select time from synthetic...	Usually as much detail as Time Study since data has usually been...	Where adequate data has been gathered usually provides a suffic...

	containing the elements concerned, or from synthetic data	(b) Calculate standard time for job	curacy depends upon amount of data available and care in application usually consistent	of determining times, often without recourse to stopwatch, and prior to starting job
(2) Pre-determined motion time systems	A work measurement technique whereby times established for basic human motions (classified according to the nature of the motion and the conditions under which it is made) are used to build up the time for a job at a defined level of performance	(1) Get all details of the job to be measured (2) Determine amount of detail required (3) Construct time for job (4) Determine allowances (5) Calculate standard time for job	Systems are available to provide various levels of detail. Consistency is ensured, and accuracy with many systems is greater than that of time study	Where consistency and accuracy are important. Detailed systems are time consuming to apply. Later systems forfeit detail for speed of application. Suitable for use amongst indirect workers and for intermittent work.
(3) Analytical estimating	A work measurement technique, being a development of estimating, whereby the time required to carry out elements of a job at a defined level of performance is estimated from knowledge and practical experience of the elements concerned	(1) Get all information concerning job to be measured (2) Divide job into elements (3) (a) Apply synthetic data where available (b) Estimate or time element durations (4) Determine allowances (5) Calculate standard time for job	Uses synthetic data supplemented by either Time Studies or estimates. Slightly less accurate and consistent than synthesis	Where insufficient synthetic data is available. Rapid method, suitable for intermittent work e.g. maintenance

Figure 73

(5) Determine *allowances*. The actual times obtained from observation, corrected for the assessed rate of working, are not necessarily the times which will be allowed for the job, since it will usually be necessary to provide allowances to cover such factors as personal needs, fatigue, contingencies, interruptions, etc. Such allowances, often derived on a basis of experience, frequently account for up to 20 per cent of the standard time.

(6) Calculate *standard time for job*. The standard time for each work element, and hence for the entire job, is calculated by using the following formula:

Standard time for element

$$= (basic \text{ time}) \times (\% \text{ total allowances})$$
$$= \left(\text{actual or observed time} \times \frac{\text{BS rating}}{100} \right) \times (\% \text{ total allowances})$$

Standard time for job $= \Sigma$ standard times for all elements in job

The major subjective feature of time study is undoubtedly that of operator rating. In rating an operator, the time-study practitioner will have recourse to one of several outline procedures to assist him, but basically he is required to compare an actual rate of working with a conceptual standard rate. The accuracy and consistency with which the observer rates the operator will, therefore, depend predominantly upon his training and experience. Similarly, however well-defined the various *types* of allowance that can be provided, the total allowances given will be at best dependent essentially upon the abilities of the observer and at worst may be largely arbitrary.

Data obtained from time studies are often collected, classified and stored for future reference. When sufficient data has been collected it is often possible to calculate formulae, draw graphs or compile tables which permit times to be constructed or synthesized for jobs, thus avoiding the need to conduct further direct time studies. Because working conditions etc. are likely to change, and because allowances are normally given for a job as a whole rather than to individual elements, this synthetic data normally relates to basic times, after rating but before the provision of allowances.

Distance moved inches	Time TMU				Hand in motion		Case and description
	A	B	C or D	E	A	B	
¾ or less	2·0	2·0	2·0	2·0	1·6	1·6	**A** Reach to object in fixed location, or to object in other hand or on which other hand rests.
1	2·5	2·5	3·6	2·4	2·3	2·3	
2	4·0	4·0	5·9	3·8	3·5	2·7	
3	5·3	5·3	7·3	5·3	4·5	3·6	
4	6·1	6·4	8·4	6·8	4·9	4·3	**B** Reach to single object in location which may vary slightly from cycle to cycle.
5	6·5	7·8	9·4	7·4	5·3	5·0	
6	7·0	8·6	10·1	8·0	5·7	5·7	**C** Reach to object jumbled with other objects in a group so that search and select occur.
7	7·4	9·3	10·8	8·7	6·1	6·5	
8	7·9	10·1	11·5	9·3	6·5	7·2	
9	8·3	10·8	12·2	9·9	6·9	7·9	
10	8·7	11·5	12·9	10·5	7·3	8·6	
12	9·6	12·9	14·2	11·8	8·1	10·1	**D** Reach to a very small object or where accurate grasp is required.
14	10·5	14·4	15·6	13·0	8·9	11·5	
16	11·4	15·8	17·0	14·2	9·7	12·9	
18	12·3	17·2	18·4	15·5	10·5	14·4	
20	13·1	18·6	19·8	16·7	11·3	15·8	
22	14·0	20·1	21·2	18·0	12·1	17·3	**E** Reach to indefinite location to get hand in position for body balance or next motion or out of way.
24	14·9	21·5	22·5	19·2	12·9	18·8	
26	15·8	22·9	23·9	20·4	13·7	20·2	
28	16·7	24·4	25·3	21·7	14·5	21·7	
30	17·5	25·8	26·7	22·9	15·3	23·2	

Figure 74 Table of Times for Reach from the MTM-1 Data Card
Reprinted by permission of the MTM Association of the United Kingdom.

The use of *predetermined motion time systems* is an increasingly important aspect of work measurement. Such systems were first designed and used about thirty years ago in America, and since then there has been continuous development. Only comparatively recently, however, have PMT systems achieved really widespread use. Perhaps the best known PMT system is *Methods Time Measurement* (MTM), developed in America and first published in 1948.* In its original form (MTM 1) this system

MTM – 2

CODE	GA	GB	GC	PA	PB	PC
−5	3	7	14	3	10	21
−15	6	10	19	6	15	26
−30	9	14	23	11	19	30
−45	13	18	27	15	24	36
−80	17	23	32	20	30	41

GW 1 – 1 Kg.   PW 1 – 5 Kg.

A	R	E	C	S	F	B
14	6	7	15	18	9	61

WARNING: Do not attempt to use this data unless you have been trained and qualified under a scheme approved by the International MTM Directorate.

Figure 75 The MTM–2 Data Card
Reprinted by permission of the MTM Association of the United Kingdom.

provides basic times for nine classes of body motion: reach, move, turn and apply pressure, grasp, release, position, disengage, eye travel and focus, and body and leg motions. Times are given in time measurement units (TMUs) equal to 0·00001 hr,

* Maynard, H. B., *et al.*, *Methods Time Measurement*, McGraw-Hill, 1948.

and each class of movement is subdivided according to type, distance, weight of object handled, etc. An example of one of the nine tables on the MTM 1 data card is shown in Figure 74.

More recent developments in PMTs have tended to be concerned with providing basic times for larger elements of work. For example, a 'second-generation' MTM system (MTM 2) has been developed in Europe which provides basic times for nine classes of hand and body motion: get(G), put(P), apply pressure(A), regrasp(R), eye action(E), crank(C), step(S), foot motion(F), and bend and arise(B). Of these classes, only two, get and put, have variable categories, and consequently only 39 times appear on the MTM 2 data card (Figure 75).

PLANT LAYOUT

The need to design the layout of an entire factory or department obviously occurs less frequently than problems concerning the modification of existing layouts or the addition of machinery to existing layouts. Despite the obvious differences in magnitude, importance and difficulty these two types of layout-planning problem are very similar, particularly as regards criteria and procedures.

The principal objective in layout planning is the maximization of productivity, which in more immediate terms is associated with maximum utilization of facilities, minimum movement of items, minimum work in progress, minimum space requirements, maximum layout flexibility. Not surprisingly there are neither mathematical nor heuristic layout planning procedures available which take account of all or even most of these objectives, and consequently layout planning decisions are normally qualitative with mathematical, or more usually, heuristic content.

Irrespective of the type of procedure adopted, the initial objectives in layout planning are normally concerned with distance (the common denominator of all spatial layouts), and in particular with the minimization of the total distance travelled by items during manufacture.

Traditional methods of layout planning are essentially qualitative, and are concerned with visual optimization, i.e. visual minimization of the total distance travelled, utilizing diagrams, two- and three-dimensional models etc. Such procedures have a great deal in common with method study; for example the flow diagram shown in Figure 76 will be recognized as a modified

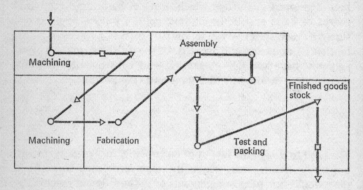

Figure 76 Flow Diagram Showing the Movement of One Item

version of a conventional flow-process chart. Because of the difficulty of both constructing and evaluating the information provided by scale models, flow diagrams, etc., it is normal when using these essentially visual methods of analysis to consider only the movement requirements of the principal products or items in planning the layout. These movement requirements in the case of a new layout will be obtained from production planning documents and in the case of an existing layout needing modification they may also be obtained by observation or activity sampling.

A useful device on which to record and present data describing inter-department or inter-machine movement is the *cross chart* (Figure 77). Each of the cells shows the extent of movement between pairs of departments, consequently the comparative size of these figures is some indication of the need to place two departments close together. Very often data collected from an

Dept. no. from \ to	1	2	3	4	5	6	7	8
1		HH HH HH 15		HH HH III 13		IIII 4		
2			III 3		HH I 6	HH I 6		
3				II 2			I 1	
4					HH 5	HH HH 10		
5						HH II 7	IIII 4	
0							HH II 7	HH HH HH HH 20
7								HH HH II 12
8								

N.B. In this case there are no entries below the diagonal since there is no 'backtracking' in item movement

Figure 77 Cross Chart

activity analysis and recorded on a cross-chart is summarized, together with other pertinent information, on a *relationship chart* which in effect shows the desirable departmental arrangement (Figure 78). The relationship chart is a useful means of summarizing requirements, but of course it is in no way a method of layout planning since, having constructed such a chart from the data and information available, it still remains for the investigator to use his skill, intuition, or trial and error to arrange the facilities in such a manner that they adequately satisfy the desired proximity requirements.

159

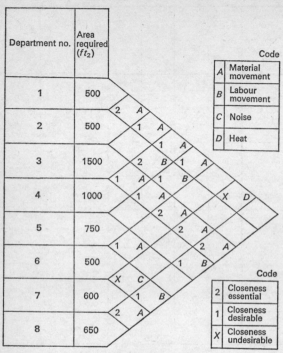

Figure 78 Relationship Chart

The usual primary objective of layout planning, i.e. the minimization of the total cost of material or item movement, can be stated as follows:

minimize total cost of movement (E)

where $E = \sum_{i=1}^{n} \sum_{j=1}^{n} d_{ij}(l_{ij}c_{ij})$

where n = number of departments

d_{ij} = distance between departments i and j

e_{ij} = number of units or items moving between departments i and j over a given period of time

c_{ij} = cost of moving one item one unit distance between departments i and j

160

Except in very simple cases methods of layout planning relying on visual analysis are unlikely to provide a reliable means of minimizing this function. Furthermore there is no adequate mathematical method available, and so we are obliged to think in terms of heuristic procedures.

There are at least five heuristic computer programs available for layout planning, all of which aim to minimize total movement or total cost of movement, and all of which have been developed specifically for computer application. These heuristic programs are of two types:

Type (1) Those designed to treat the whole problem, i.e.:

Main inputs (a) inter-departmental movement requirements in the form of cross charts giving l_{ij} and c_{ij}
(b) departmental areas

Main outputs (a) layout diagram
(b) the total movement distance and cost associated with the layout

Because this type of program deals only with material or item movement, it is specifically intended for planning the layout of production departments.

Type (2) Those designed to construct a layout which best satisfies stated desirable inter-departmental proximities, i.e.:

Main inputs (a) relationship chart
(b) departmental areas

Main outputs (a) layout diagram

Unlike the previous type of program those in this category deal only with a part (the most difficult part) of the layout planning problem, i.e. the planning of a layout from a given desirable relationship. Since in this case the input is in the form of a relationship chart, this type of program can be used to arrange both production and non-production departments.

CRAFT* (Computerized Relative Allocation of Facilities

* G. C. Armour, E. S. Buffa, 'A Heuristic Algorithm and Simulation Approach to Relative Location of Facilities', *Management Science*, IX, 2, 1963.

Technique) is a 'type 1' program which requires as input an initial layout configuration and matrices or cross charts giving inter-department movement and movement cost data. A flow diagram for the program is given in Figure 79. The program calculates the effects on the total cost of movement (E) of the interchange of pairs of departments. When an interchange is

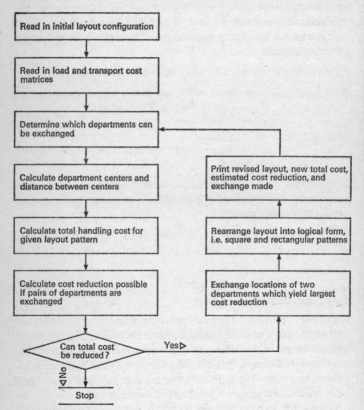

Figure 79 Flow Diagram for the CRAFT Programme Reprinted by permission from G. C. Armour, E. S. Buffa, 'A Heuristic Algorithm and Simulation Approach to Relative Location of Facilities', *Management Science*, Vol. 9, No. 2, 1963.

found which reduces E, the change is made, and the procedure repeated until no further changes are available to reduce E, whereupon the final layout is printed out.

CORELAP * (COmputerized RElationship LAyout Planning) is an example of the second type of program. In this case the heuristic program constructs or builds a layout, which grows in much the same way that a crystal grows in a solution. The program places in the centre of the layout the most 'related' department, i.e. that department which, according to the relationship chart, has the highest 'closeness rating' with all the other departments.

Around this department are placed those departments which must be close to it, and next to these are placed those departments which must be close to them, and so on until all departments feature in the layout.

PRODUCTION PLANNING AND CONTROL

Resource Allocation

The use of network analysis in production planning was discussed in Chapter 4. In dealing with this technique we discussed activity or job durations and their costs and showed that the two are inversely related, since at additional cost more resources may be applied, and thus the duration of jobs reduced. Consideration of resources availability is therefore an essential feature of production planning. If resources availability is neglected during production planning then it is conceivable that impractical plans and schedules will result. If schedule completion dates and activity durations are considered in isolation then we may at a later date find that the resources required to maintain the required schedule are not available. For example, Figure 80 is a *resource aggregation* showing the amount of one resource, say labour, required during each of several future periods in order to satisfy

* R. C. Lee, J. M. Moore, 'CORELAP – Computerized Relationship Layout Planning', *Journal of Industrial Engineering*, XVIII ,3, pp. 195–200, 1967.

a previously established schedule. In two periods, weeks number 3 and 6, the resources required exceeds the resources available. In such circumstances three possibilities are available:

Arrange to provide additional resources during the period(s) in question, e.g. by subcontracting work.

Modify the schedule in order to avoid such overloads.

Do nothing and hope that before these periods arrive the schedule will change and the overload be removed or reduced.

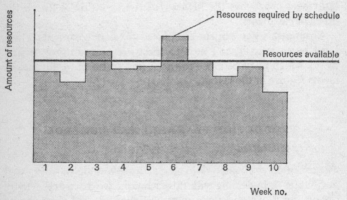

Figure 80 Resource Aggregation

Certainly occasions do arise which cause production schedules to be changed, but in the case of resource aggregations showing overloads in the near future, as in the case shown in Figure 80, it would be unwise to rely upon such unforeseen changes. Very often, therefore, one of the first two policies must be adopted and in both cases the problem is one of *resource allocation*. In the case of the first policy the decision will be influenced by the availability of suitable subcontractors. Alternatively it may be possible to arrange for a temporary increase in the level of resources available by taking on additional workers or by hiring equipment. In the case of the second policy the problem is one of deciding which jobs to schedule during each period. It is neces-

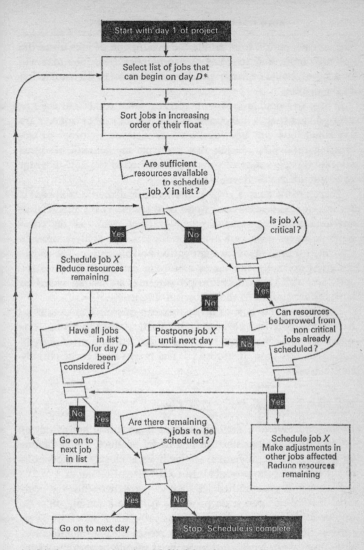

Start with day 1 of project

Select list of jobs that can begin on day D*

Sort jobs in increasing order of their float

Are sufficient resources available to schedule job X in list?

Yes

No

Is job X critical?

Schedule Job X Reduce resources remaining

No

Yes

Can resources be borrowed from non critical jobs already scheduled?

Have all jobs in list for day D been considered?

Postpone job X until next day

No

No

Yes

Go on to next job in list

Are there remaining jobs to be scheduled?

Schedule job X Make adjustments in other jobs affected Reduce resources remaining

Yes

No

Go on to next day

Stop. Schedule is complete

*day D is day under consideration; job X is job under consideration

Figure 81 Heuristic Programme for Resource Allocation

Reprinted by permission from J. D. Weist, 'Heuristic Programs for Decision Making', *Harvard Business Review*, Vol. 44, No. 5, 1966, pp. 129–43.

sary in each period to schedule the production of jobs up to the resource limit, and to delay the remainder. The jobs that will be delayed should be those which are not critical to the completion of the project.

Wherever possible jobs with zero or small total float are not delayed, and so for each period in which insufficient resources are available, jobs will be withdrawn or delayed in order of decreasing total float. Using this principle an heuristic resource allocation programme of the type described in the flow diagram in Figure 81 can be developed.

There are of course several mathematical methods available for resource allocation, but none of these are really practical in anything other than very simple situations. Many of the computer packages which are available for network analysis provide a facility for both resource aggregation and allocation. The aggregation is normally calculated assuming earliest start dates for activities, whilst the allocation programmes are usually based on a procedure similar to that shown in Figure 81.

The logic of this type of procedure can of course be criticized, but for all practical purposes, and particularly when one considers probable inaccuracies in the initial estimation of activity durations, this type of procedure has been found to be entirely satisfactory.

The Design of Assembly or Flow Lines

In mass production, facilities layout is an important aspect of production planning, since in layout by product, unlike layout by process, the arrangement of facilities is closely related both to the nature of the product and to the size of demand.

Except in process industries such as petrochemicals, the principal feature of large scale production is the assembly, flow or production line which consists basically of a series of *work stations* through which the product passes during manufacture. Very often these work stations consist of one or more workers each responsible for performing one small part of the total work content of the job. Occasionally work stations consist only of machines working on an automatic cycle, and in this case, especially when the movement of items from one station to the next is automatic, the line is known as a *transfer line*.

The person responsible for designing an assembly line is usually equipped with information concerning:

(a) The product to be made, particularly the total work content involved, i.e.:

$$\text{Total work content} = \sum_{i=1}^{m} t_i$$

where t_i = standard time for work element i

m = total number of work elements

and (b) the quantity to be produced in a given time (N).

Two of the most important tasks in designing such a line are, firstly, determining the number of work stations required, and secondly, allocating work to each of these stations. The minimum number of stations (n_{min}) can be calculated as follows:

$$n_{min} = \frac{N \sum_{i=1}^{m} t_i}{T}$$

where N = number of items to be produced in T amount of time.

Because of limitations on the way in which the total work content of any job may be divided, the actual number of stations required, n, will usually be greater than n_{min}.

The rate at which items must be produced by the line, which is determined by N and T, will determine the amount of time known as the cycle time (c) available at each work station. In allocating work to each station the objectives are to achieve a balance, that is to give as nearly as possible the same amount of work to each station, and to allocate to each station an amount of work equal to the cycle time. The latter is rarely possible and consequently a certain amount of inefficiency arises which is known as *balancing loss*. The balancing loss is equal to the difference between the total work content of the job and the sum of the cycle times for all stations expressed as a percentage, i.e.

$$\% \text{ balancing loss} = \frac{\left(n(c) - \sum_{i=1}^{m} t_i\right)}{n(c)} \times 100$$

This whole process of dividing the total work content of a job between the necessary number of work stations is known as *line balancing*, and represents one of the major fields of application of heuristic procedures in production management.

The way in which the total work content of a job can be divided between stations is determined largely by:

The size of the work elements which constitute the job

The order in which these elements of work must be performed

Any limitations imposed on the grouping of elements, e.g. the need to have certain elements at the same station because of their use of special equipment etc.

Several mathematical procedures have been proposed and developed for solving assembly line balancing problems but, because of limitations of size, these are rarely if ever used in practice. About a dozen heuristic methods have been developed, many of which form the basis of the procedures used widely in industry. As an illustration of the use of heuristics in this context we will describe, very briefly, one such method, first developed in 1961 and known as the *ranked positional weight technique*.[*]

Figure 82 is a precedence diagram showing the order in which the elements of work, which together constitute a small job, must be performed. The figures above the circles representing the elements are the element durations (hours) which will have been obtained by work measurement. Figure 83 is a list of elements showing the number of succeeding elements and giving also the 'positional weight' of each element. The positional weight (PW) is calculated as follows:

$$PW \text{ for element} = \frac{\text{duration}}{\text{of element}} + \frac{\text{duration of } all}{\text{succeeding elements}}$$

---

[*] W. B. Helgeson, D. P. Birnie, 'Assembly Line Balancing Using the Ranked Positional Weight Technique', *Journal of Industrial Engineering*, Vol. XVII, No. 6, 1961.

The positional weight of an element is a measure of the size of the element, and its position in the precedence chart. Logically it should be our intention to allocate firstly those elements which

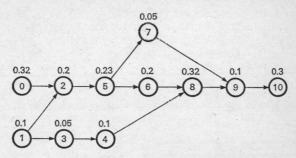

Figure 82 Element Precedence Diagram

Reproduced by permission from Ray Wild, *The Techniques of Production Management,* Holt, Rinehart & Winston, 1970.

are large (i.e. allocate the large elements to stations whilst there is sufficient time available to accommodate them) and/or those which occur early in the precedence diagram (i.e. if we allocate

Element no.	Succeeding elements	Positional weight of element
0	2, 5, 6, 7, 8, 9, 10	1·72
1	2, 3, 4, 5, 6, 7, 8, 9, 10	1·65
2	5, 6, 7, 8, 9, 10	1·40
3	4, 8, 9, 10	0·87
4	8, 9, 10	0·82
5	6, 7, 8, 9, 10	1·20
6	8, 9, 10	0·92
7	9, 10	0·45
8	9, 10	0·72
9	10	0·40
10	—	0·30

Figure 83

such elements to stations as soon as possible we will avoid delaying those elements which succeed them). In other words we should attempt to allocate elements to stations in order of descending positional weight. The procedure to be followed, therefore, can be summarized as follows:

For work station No. 1:
   (a) Allocate element with highest PW if:
      (i) this does not violate any precedence requirements.
   (b) Allocate remaining element with highest PW if:
      (i) this does not violate any precedence requirements.
      (ii) there is sufficient time available at the station to accommodate this element.
   if not: repeat (b)
   until: none of the remaining elements can be allocated at station, then:

For work station No. 2:
   (a) Allocate remaining element with highest PW, if:
      (i) this does not violate any precedence requirement.
      (ii) there is sufficient time available at the station to accommodate this element.
   if not: repeat (a)
   until: none of the remaining elements can be allocated at station, then:
Continue for subsequent work stations until all elements are allocated.

The allocation of elements to stations for the example shown in Figures 82 and 83 is given in Figure 84. Four stations are required to satisfy a given output equal to a cycle time of 0·55 hrs, and the balancing loss is 10·4 per cent.

Dispatching

One intriguing characteristic of intermittent, particularly jobbing, production is the occurrence of two equally undesirable states: high work in progress and the underutilization of manufacturing facilities. This somewhat paradoxical situation is of course accompanied by long production times for items, often many times greater than the total operation time required.

In operational research terms, jobbing production is an interesting example of a complex queueing situation, since at most

Work station	Element	PW	Immediate predecessor	Element time	Cumulative station time (X)	Unassigned station time (C − X)
	0	1·72	—	0·32	0·32	0·23
1	1	1·65	—	0·1	0·42	0·13
	3	0·87	1	0·05	0·47	0·08
	2	1·4	0, 1	0·2	0·2	0·35
2	5	1·2	2	0·23	0·43	0·12
	4	0·82	3	0·1	0·53	0·02
3	6	0·92	5	0·2	0·2	0·35
	8	0·72	4, 6	0·32	0·52	0·03
	7	0·45	5	0·05	0·05	0·50
4	9	0·4	7, 8	0·1	0·15	0·40
	10	0·3	9	0·3	0·45	0·10

$$C = 0.55$$

$$\text{Balancing loss} = \frac{4(0.55) - 1.97}{4(0.55)} \times 100 = 10.4\%$$

Figure 84 Element Allocation for Cycle Time of 0.35 hrs

Reproduced by permission from Ray Wild, *The Techniques of Production Management,* Holt, Rinehart & Winston, 1970.

machines long queues of jobs will often exist, whilst others will be idle because of a lack of jobs requiring those types of operation. This unfortunate situation occurs because of a lack of balance at any one time between the amount of facilities required and the

171

amount of facilities available. However, because the number and nature of facilities required is liable to change substantially and frequently, it is unreasonable to expect a perfect balance to be achieved, except instantaneously.

This type of situation gives rise to some particularly difficult management problems, and one of the most important to the production manager is the dispatching problem, concerned with the decision as to which of the several jobs available at a machine will be processed when that machine becomes available.

Because the dispatching problem is dynamic rather than static, i.e. because jobs will continually join the queue at any machine, there is little point in determining the processing order for the entire queue since their relative priorities may change as new jobs arrive. The dispatching decision, therefore, normally involves calculation only when the machine becomes vacant, in order to determine which job *at that time* has highest priority. If for any reason a static situation exists, then it becomes feasible to think in terms of the correct order for *all* jobs; furthermore on occasions one must attempt to determine the optimum order for several jobs on several machines. This latter situation is known as the *sequencing* problem. Numerous mathematical algorithms have been developed for the solution of the sequencing problems but in practice such techniques are rarely used, and many of them are relevant only to somewhat abstract and unrealistic situations.

In principle the dispatching decision is concerned with the determination of a queue discipline, or the allocation of priorities to the items waiting in a queue. Dispatching decisions are normally based on heuristically derived *priority rules*. For example operation start dates are determined during production planning, and it clearly makes sense to use such dates to establish priorities for jobs during production control. Network analysis calculations produce two start dates for each operation – the 'earliest' and 'latest start' dates. The earliest start date, sometimes called the planned start date, is frequently used for dispatching purposes in conjunction with the total float value. In other words, the priority rule used by the production controller to establish the queue discipline is as follows: 'Process first the job with the earliest planned start date, and in the case of "ties" process first the job with least total float.' This is an example of a *compound* priority rule, consisting of two parts – planned start date and total float. Simple priority rules consist of one part only. The following are examples:

(1) Scheduled or planned start date
   i.e. process first the job with the earliest scheduled start date for this operation.
(2) Number of remaining operations
   i.e. process first the job with the greatest number of remaining operations.
(3) Due date
   i.e. schedule first the job with the earliest scheduled completion date.

Priority rules may also be classified as follows:

(a) *Local rules* which depend solely upon the data relating to the jobs in the queue at any one time. Each of the three rules above are local rules.

(b) *General rules* which depend also upon data relating to jobs in the queues at other machines. The following is an example of a general priority rule:

(4) Subsequent operation
   i.e. process first the job which after this operation goes to the shortest queue, thus minimizing the possibility of machine idle time.

(c) *Dynamic rules*, where the priority given to a job is a function of time. The following is a dynamic priority rule:

(5) Job slack
   i.e. Process first the job with the least amount of contingency or free time over and above the processing time required. Job slack (S) is calculated as follows:
   $$S = t_o - t_i - \Sigma a_i$$
   where t_i = present date
   t_o = due date for job
   Σa_i = sum of processing times for all remaining operations on job.

173

(d) *Static rules*, such as 1, 2 and 3 above, where the priority is not directly dependent upon time.

(e) *Random rules* where the priority given to a job does not depend upon pertinent characteristics such as the number of operations, scheduled dates etc. The following are random priority rules:

(6) Job number
   i.e. process first the job with the largest job number.
(7) First come first served
   i.e. process first the job which was first to arrive at the machine.

Every production control system used in jobbing or small batch manufacturing industries depends upon some type of priority rule for dispatching. Consider for example, the rather extreme situation in which formal production control is completely absent. In such a case the dispatching decisions will be made either by the machine operators or by their supervisors. In either case the decision will be influenced by their knowledge of the urgency of the job and by various other factors such as the piecework price afforded by the job, or its physical size and the resulting inconvenience or danger associated with its storage. In other situations the priority attached to jobs awaiting processing may be influenced by the actions, particularly the complaints, of the customer or by requests from other manufacturing departments presently waiting for the job.

Many production control systems depend very largely upon the abilities of people known as *progress chasers* whose job it is to see that certain items (perhaps those associated with one particular contract, or all items in a particular production area) progress through their respective operations with as little delay as possible, and that the production of certain interdependent items is coordinated. In such cases dispatching decisions may depend entirely or largely upon their judgement or even upon their influence with production supervisors and operators.

Whatever the situation, dispatching decisions will be based upon certain, perhaps continually changing, priority criteria, whether subjective or objective, rational or irrational.

The use of priority rules such as those described in Figure 85 is in no way a radical concept. The development of these heuristics is merely an attempt to formalize normal dispatching practice with the objective of providing consistent and efficient dispatching

Rule		*Explanation*
(1) First come, first served	(FCFS)	See text – Rule 7
(2) Last come, first served	(LCFS)	Reverse of FCFS
(3) First in system, first served	(FISFS)	Process first the job on which production started first
(4) Shortest imminent operation	(SIO)	Process first the job with the shortest operation time
(5) Longest imminent operation	(LIO)	Process first the job with the longest operation time
(6) SIO, 2 class rule		Use FCFS within each of 2 classes defined by operation time
(7) SIO, with truncation		Use SIO rule, but give priority to those jobs which have waited more than a given time
(8) SIO/FCFS		Use SIO, and FCFS alternately
(9) Job slack (or dynamic slack)	(DS)	See text – Rule 5
(10) Job slack per operation	(DS/O)	DS divided by number of remaining operations
(11) Job slack per remaining process time	(DS/P)	DS divided by sum of remaining operation times
(12) Due date	(D)	See text – Rule 3
(13) Subsequent operation	(SO)	See text – Rule 4
(14) Static slack	(SS)	Due date minus time of arrival into queue
(15) Static slack per operation	(SS/O)	SS divided by number of remaining operations
(16) Number of remaining operations		See text – Rule 2
(17) Amount of work remaining		
(18) Random		
(19) Scheduled start date		See text – Rule 1

Figure 85 A Selection of Dispatching Priority Rules

decisions. Most of the priority rules given in the figure appear to be intuitively logical, but mere examination does not of course reveal anything about their suitability or performance, which can only be established empirically. A great deal of research has been undertaken with the purpose of examining the 'performance' of priority rules in various situations. Almost all of this research has utilized simulation methods, a digital computer being used to construct models of jobbing shops having varying numbers of machines with varying work loads. Numerous criteria have been used to assess the performance of these rules, the following being perhaps the most widely used:

Flow time criteria, concerned with the speed with which a job is completed:

(a) Mean flow time – average time to process a job

(b) Flow time variance – a measure of the variability about mean time

Due date criteria, concerned with whether or not they are completed by previously specified 'due' or scheduled completion dates:

(a) Mean of the completion time distribution

(b) The variance of the completion distribution

(c) Number of jobs late

(d) Mean lateness

Work in progress and congestion criteria:

(a) Work remaining – sum of the processing times of all operations not yet completed

(b) Mean number of jobs in shop

(c) Variance of number of jobs in shop

(d) Total work content – sum of the processing times of all operations of all jobs in the shop

The amount of research work conducted in this area, and the fact that few of the individual studies are truly comparable as regards the details of the production system that they have simulated, makes generalization hazardous. However, there do appear to be certain discernible issues on which there is more or less general agreement which may be summarized as follows:

The most effective simple rule is undoubtedly the shortest imminent operation rule. Earlier research appeared to indicate that the principal disadvantage of this rule was its poor performance on the flow time variance criteria, but recently it has been found that these suspicions were largely unfounded. There are several variations on the simple SIO rule, many of which were derived to improve the rule's flow time variance performance. With a few exceptions these derivations offer improved 'all-round' performance, particularly those which involve use of SIO in conjunction with a 'look-ahead' heuristic. The 'two-class' and the 'truncated' SIO rules have also been found to provide good dispatching performances.

READING REFERENCES

Aronofsky, J. S. (Ed.), *Progress in Operations Research* Vol. III, Ch. 10, Wiley, 1969.

BS 3138 – 1959, British Standards Institute, London.

Currie, R. M., *Work Study*, Pitman, 1968.

Hertz, D. B., Eddison, R. T. (Eds.), *Progress in Operations Research,* Vol. II, Ch. 5, Wiley, 1964.

Larkin, J. A., *Work Study – Theory and Practice*, McGraw-Hill, 1969.

Moore, J. M., Wilson, R. C., 'A Review of Simulation Research in Job Shop Scheduling', *Production and Inventory Management*, Jan. 1967, pp. 1–10.

Muther, R. M., *Systematic Layout Planning*, Industrial Education Institute, Boston, Mass., 1961.

Muther, R. M., McPherson, K., 'Four Approaches to Computerized Layout Planning', *Industrial Engineering*, Feb. 1970, pp. 39–42.

Weist, J. D., 'Heuristic Programs for Decision-Making', *Harvard Business Review*, Sept.–Oct. 1966, pp. 129–43.

Wild, R., *The Techniques of Production Management*, Holt, Rinehart and Winston, 1970.

CHAPTER 7

Computers in Production Management

As little as a decade ago, comparatively few companies were using electronic digital computers,* and commercial or industrial applications of such machines were rare. Ten or fifteen years ago computers were fragile, often temperamental, machines; they were difficult to program and had little or no ability to digest instructions written in English; they were slow by present-day standards, had small storage capacities and slow input/output channels; and they were used largely as 'number-crunching' calculating machines for research purposes.

During the last ten years the nature of computers, the manner in which they are used, the number of installations, and their influence on commercial and industrial operations have changed almost beyond recognition. Over the past ten years the number of computers in the world has risen from approximately 3,000 to over 75,000. In the United Kingdom the number of computer installations has trebled over the past three years, and the present total of 4,500 is expected to increase to 10,000 by 1975. Fifteen years ago it was rare for a company to have its own computer installation, but nowadays it is not unusual for a large company fully to utilize an installation consisting of several powerful machines.

The influence of computers in production, as in every other facet of business, has been substantial, yet it is likely that present applications barely scratch the surface of the potential influence of such machines in these areas.

The amount of computing time devoted to production problems is probably increasing at an exponential rate, and descriptions

* Fundamentally there are three types of computer: electronic digital (used extensively in industrial and commercial applications), analog (largely special-purpose scientific machinery), and hybrid (a combination of the other two types). Throughout this chapter we shall be referring to electronic digital machines, unless specifically stated otherwise.

of proposed and actual applications which would have been dismissed as pure fantasy a decade ago now appear at frequent intervals. Many aspects of production management are now the established (almost traditional) domain of digital computers, and few problem areas are unexplored although many remain substantially unaffected. In this chapter we can only attempt to deal briefly with an extensive and important subject, and so we must confine our discussion to some of the more proven areas of application.

PRODUCTION AND INVENTORY PLANNING AND CONTROL

In 1967 the National Computing Laboratory conducted a survey of companies using computers in this field of application. The statistics in Figure 86 derived from that investigation indicate how and where these companies were using computers.

Activity heading	Percentage of companies
Order entry processing	65
Stock control	83
Demand breakdown	68
Bulk load forward production planning	55
Shop production schedule	78
Critical path scheduling	13
Shop documentation	83
Feed back data collection	80
Work progress control	68
Progress control on purchasing	43
Analysis of utilization of resources	38
Costing of production	50

Figure 86 The Use of Computers in Production Management

Data from NCL Survey, 1967

We can distinguish between two areas of planning and control in which computers find widespread applications. Firstly the field covered by Figure 86, involving the planning and timing of operations including scheduling, loading, stock control, dispatching, and progress reporting during production. As we have

179

pointed out in an earlier chapter this type of planning and control is particularly difficult in jobbing production where, because of the complexity of the situation and the need to process large quantities of information, computer-based or -assisted planning and control is particularly appropriate. The second field of application will be referred to as *process control* and involves the actual, often direct, 'on-line'* control of production operations by the computer. The classic examples of such applications can be found in capital-intensive process industries such as chemicals, steel-making, refining etc., where computers are often used continuously to monitor the performance of the plant, and either directly or indirectly to control the process operations.

Job Shop Planning and Control

For purposes of illustration, we will consider a manufacturing company producing items in small or unit quantities to customer order, using a small or medium sized computer having punched card input and magnetic tape storage facilities. In these circumstances the planning and control procedures might operate in the following manner (see Figure 87). When an order comes into the company it is checked in order to establish whether the product required has been manufactured previously. If so the order number, the quantity and delivery required and the part or product number are punched onto a card. This information, together with the same information for all other orders received, is fed into the computer which produces or amends the finished part-production programme. A list of assemblies, parts and materials required for the orders is prepared by reference to a master parts-breakdown list. This bill of requirements is compared with the available stock levels, and items which are not available for stock are entered on a forward requirements list. Using the work-in-progress and forward plant-load file and master routing requirements, detailed production schedules and shop documentation

* We shall refer to an on-line application as involving a direct linkage of equipment to the computer without intermediate processing, storage or delay.

(e.g. stores requisitions, job cards etc.) are produced. In addition purchase requirements are produced, together with machine load summaries, etc. The shop documentation is used in feeding back production progress information. When production operations are completed job tickets are either returned manually to the production control department where they are loaded into a card reader and are used to update the work-in-progress file, or alternatively read by remote data-collection terminals placed on the shop floor, and used with data concerning scrap rates, completion times, etc., for the same purpose. Stores requisition and issue cards may be used in a similar manner to update stock records. Additionally the computer will be used to produce loading instructions showing the order in which jobs are to be started on each machine, or in each machine area. Stock exception reports and progress summaries will also be produced together with forward aggregate production requirements, purchase requirements, and lists of overdue items, jigs and tools lists, etc.

In essence the design of such a planning and control system is simple and various additions or modifications may be included depending upon the requirements of specific circumstances. In practice, however, an effective system of the type described above is often surprisingly difficult to establish, largely because of the need to create accurate and comprehensive master files. Any computer-based production planning or control system depends upon the use of master files of basic reference data such as parts lists, stock lists, operations routing instructions, capacity lists, etc. Such files are the core of any computer-based system, and consequently it is imperative that they should be as accurate and comprehensive as possible. They must be regularly and accurately updated, and safeguards must be established to detect and eliminate the errors which inevitably occur. The practical problems of creating and maintaining such files are considerable. It is by no means uncommon to find that the information required for the files does not exist as a formal body of knowledge but is distributed throughout the organization in numerous documents, books and memories. Often data are of questionable accuracy and various records are found to be in apparent conflict. Even

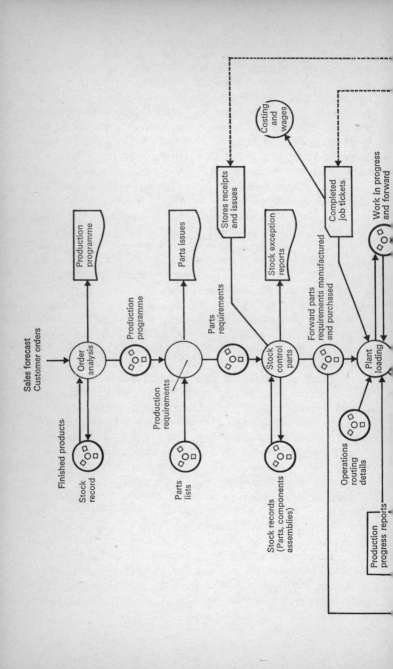

Sales forecast
Customer orders

Finished products.

Production programme

Production programme

Parts issues

Stores receipts and issues

Stock exception reports

Costing and wages

Completed job tickets

Work in progress and forward

Order analysis

Stock record

Production requirements

Parts lists

Parts requirements

Stock control parts

Stock records (Parts, components assemblies)

Forward parts requirements manufactured and purchased

Operations routing details

Plant loading

Production progress reports

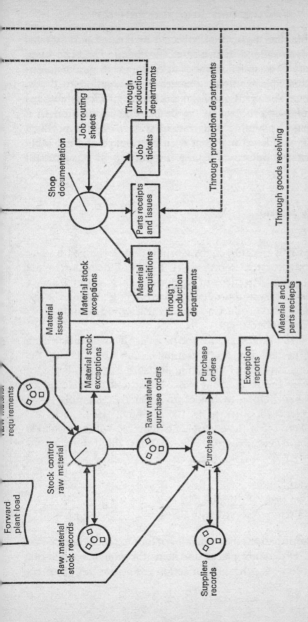

Figure 87 Reproduced by permission from Ray Wild, *The Techniques of Production Management*, Holt, Rinehart & Winston, 1970.

when reliable data have been collected or created and systems have been designed and implemented for updating and checking, it is necessary to establish methods of dealing with modifications to design and specifications, changes in production methods, materials, etc. The creation and maintenance of files is perhaps the most difficult problem in the design and installation of a computer-based planning and control system. It is a problem which is often underestimated or even overlooked and probably accounts for the failure of a large proportion of unsuccessful systems.

Examples of Systems

EXAMPLE 1

In the mid 1960s the Burroughs Corporation developed a planning and control system known as ACTION at their Electrodata Division factory at Pasadena in California. Their objectives were to control inventory and production more tightly, to end the use of manual files, and produce a system which would automatically spotlight danger conditions.

At the centre of the system is the parts list file which lists each component needed for every computer assembly. Using the file, periodic print-outs of the components used are produced, to be checked by the engineering department and updated as indicated by them. Upon receipt of an order the assembly is exploded into its component parts, the computer then checks the inventory file to see if the components required will be available when needed. The inventory file contains the following information:

Quantity on hand
Quantity on order, with due dates
Quantity already reserved with dates

Using this information, the available balance for each date can be determined. Orders are placed for items for which a stock-out condition is forecast, through an action requisition notice or reorder notice which is printed together with the dates and quantity needed. These notice cards are sent to either the production planning or purchasing departments who later return them, thus indicating that the necessary action has been taken.

The process for receiving and inspecting components is similarly coordinated by the computer. Upon receipt of an item a receiving report card is input to the computer which updates the inventory file. The parts then proceed to the inspection department which reports via a terminal to the computer department when a lot fails its acceptance tests. In the case of bought-out parts reorder and rejection notices are immediately sent, whilst in the case of made-in parts the parts are sent to the salvage department. The salvage department report their findings (i.e. whether to rework or scrap) back to the computer which then takes the appropriate action by updating its working files and issuing the necessary reorder to the production department.

The production of a computer assembly is controlled in a similar way. Before the job is released to the shop floor, cards are punched listing the parts needed and the inspection stages to be passed. As parts are withdrawn from stock the cards are surrendered to the stock control department and they are used to update inventory files. The inspection cards are similarly returned when inspection stages are completed, and thus the progress of a job through assembly can be followed.

In the inventory file system a special exception routine is utilized to highlight potential danger spots. For example, fourteen days before parts are due to be issued to the shop floor, the inventory files are scanned to establish whether the parts are in stock. The potential shortage report allows the production control department to decide whether to expedite parts or delay the job for which they are required. Figure 88 describes the entire Inventory–Production system developed by Burroughs.

Burroughs claim the following advantages for their system.

Although buying has increased five times, the number of clerical staff has fallen.

Although production too has increased five times inventories have fallen by a quarter.

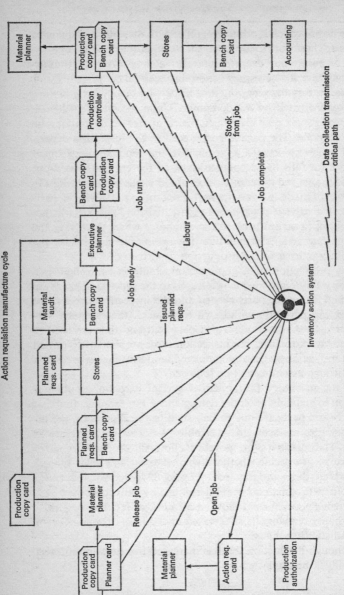

Figure 88 Above Diagram Illustrates Entire Inventory-Production System Developed by Burroughs

Reproduced by permission from R. M. Smith, 'Automated Production-Inventory Control', *Management Services,* Sept./Oct. 1965, pp. 18–25.

Two million dollars per annum are saved by better inventory control, permitting the use of blanket purchasing contracts.

They have immediately available a total inventory and order information file. They can also determine the total demand on the factory at any one point in time.

EXAMPLE 2

The CAV company manufacture electrical and diesel equipment for vehicles. Their output consists of approximately 4,000 different products together utilizing 100,000 different components. All products are made to order, but a stock of 30,000 different spare parts is maintained.

At the centre of the CAV computer system is a master file listing the 100,000 components, indicating where they are used and the operations and times required for their manufacture. A stock file lists the parts available in the warehouse, and the orders that have been received from customers. A third file contains the details of production equipment, plant capacity etc.

Every month the sales plan is entered and exploded to its component parts – the demand for each part being netted at each manufacturing level. To this plan is added the demand from stores for spare parts; this demand figure is determined by exponential smoothing. The computer then lists the machine types and capacity required and by reference to the present status of the shop indicates bottlenecks, and possible alternative manufacturing routes.

Production and stock status is updated regularly using information obtained either from the foremen or automatically from each machine.

EXAMPLE 3

A somewhat different set of planning and control problems face companies involved in the manufacture of large complex items for which throughput time is high. One such company is the British Aircraft Corporation, whose chief problem was one of product size. For example there are approximately 250,000 parts in a VC-10 aircraft, and one aircraft takes approximately eighteen months to construct. To help deal with production planning and control problems in such a situation, BAC designed their own production control system, appropriately named EPIC (engineering and production information control).

To reduce the problem to manageable proportions they divided the assembly period into a number of time stages. They were helped in this by the nature of aircraft construction, which requires many final assemblies. The production problem was then viewed as a series of stages, each stage effectively an end product in itself.

The production control system adopted was fairly conventional; the program nets the demand for components against work-in-progress stock. In the case of low-value components orders are placed in economic batch quantities, but high-value items are ordered only as required.

One important problem in aircraft construction derives from the fact that the design of the end product is subject to change because of continuing research and different customer requirements. Thus there are problems of file maintenance, particularly in respect of the gross requirements master file.

The system provides for the monitoring of work centres to provide up to date information on shop and job status; and also a vendor monitoring system, to check if subcontracted parts will be delivered on time. There is also a tool control file detailing the capacity of machines and jigs; consequently EPIC takes into account problems of resource restrictions and attempts to avoid overloads and delays by simple methods of production scheduling.

EXAMPLE 4

The Parsons Marine Turbine Company was faced by a similar problem to that of BAC: a two-year manufacturing makespan. The basic inputs to the computer-based system which was designed to deal with this situation are details of job activities and routes, a contract information file, and a job and shop status file, both of the latter two files updated weekly.

The system is based on the network analysis principle; activity scheduling influenced by scheduled start and finish dates, criticality, and resource limitations. Activities with non-critical resources are scheduled at their earliest dates and those with critical resources are delayed until they can be fitted in without overloading. The weekly outputs from the system consist of work centre schedules for the next twenty working days, resource load summaries for each department, a contract schedule summary (showing activities with negative slack), and a list of resources needed for assemblies. A report which predicts contract completion dates, a two-year resource load summary, and a two-year forecast of the firm's revenues and profits are produced less frequently.

Process Control

There are three basic types of process control application, namely:
Data Logging. This is the simplest type of application, in which the process control computer is used to scan rapidly and frequently, the information displayed by or provided by several instruments such as transducers, thermometers, flowmeters, etc. This information would normally be printed out for the benefit of those whose job it is to ensure the efficient operation of the system. Such an installation is therefore an application of the 'open-loop' control principle in which the control of the process is not associated directly with the sensory feature, but via an intermediary. In other words the computer does not exercise direct control over the process.

Supervisory Control Systems. One of the principal disadvantages of data logging systems is the time lag or delay in the sensing/evaluating/control cycle. In many complex installations such delays cannot be tolerated either because of financial penalties or because of safety hazards arising from the temporary maladjustment of the process. In such circumstances manual control is undesirable, and consequently it is necessary to provide a close-loop control system in which the monitoring of performance and the necessary adjustment to the process are under the control of a suitably designed and programmed computer.

Direct Digital Control (DDC). DDC is an extension of

supervisory control, the principal difference being that the latter system utilizes analog controllers between process and computer, whereas DDC effects control of the process without the use of conventional analog controllers.

In many of the early process-control applications of computers analog machines were used; the conventional present-day application incorporates a purpose-designed digital machine. Such process-control computers consist of:

A memory unit – to store data
An arithmetic unit – to perform calculations
A control unit – to coordinate each of the other units
An input unit – to obtain data from the process
An output unit – to transmit 'instructions' to the process
The operators' unit – to enable the operators to communicate with the computer

A block diagram showing the interrelation of these various units is shown in Figure 89.

Data obtained from scanning and reading devices is passed to the computer where they are interpreted and evaluated. As a result of such evaluation, the extent of any adjustments to the process controls are established. The installation requires a digital clock to bring the control system into operation and an ordered system of control loops which amongst other things determines priorities when several adjustments are to be made. Figure 90 describes the logic of such a process-control loop.

The world's first DDC installation was at the Fleetwood plant of ICI Ltd, where in 1962 a process-control computer was used to control ninety valves in the soda ash plant. Since that date very many DDC installations have been brought into service throughout the world. In the United Kingdom perhaps the best examples are to be found in the steel industry, where installations tend to be both complex and comprehensive, often utilizing a hierarchy of computers to exercise control over sequentially dependent processes. For example, Figure 91 shows diagrammatically how process control was achieved at the Park Gate Iron and Steel Company at Rotherham. Work on the design of the installation was begun in 1961, commissioning commenced in 1963, and the installation came into service in 1964, since which date development work has continued. This installation, in its original form,

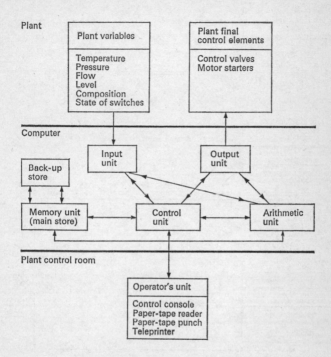

Figure 89 Block Diagram of a DDC System
Reproduced by permission from M. S. Beck, N. Wainwright, 'Direct Digital Control of Chemical Processes', *Control,* Sept. 1967.

is an example of integrated process control, in which three ICL, KDN2 computers were used in the system which covered overall production planning as well as planning and control of the operations in the primary and finishing mills. Overall production planning was undertaken on one off-line computer with the other two machines used on-line.

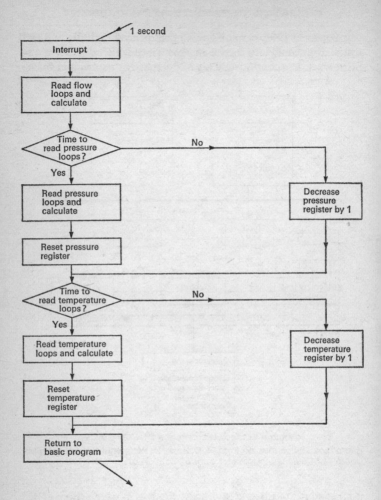

Figure 90 Executive Sub-routine for Control Calculations
Reproduced by permission from Beck, Wainwright, op. cit.

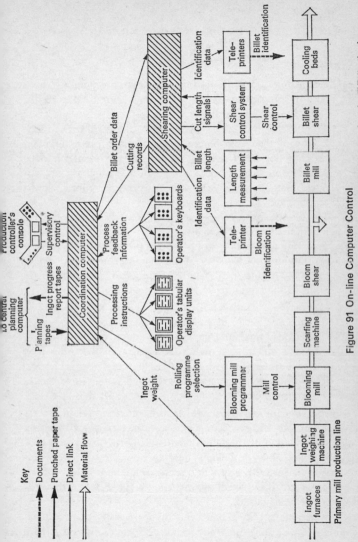

Figure 91 On-line Computer Control

Reproduced by permission from G. H. Kelly, 'Integrated Computer Control of Steelworks Production', *English Electric Journal*, Vol. 19, No. 4, 1964.

STOCK PLANNING, CONTROL AND HANDLING

Computers have found application in stock planning and control in three basic areas:

(1) Recording stock transactions, e.g. where pre-punched cards read by remote data-collection terminals are used to record stock receipts and issues

(2) The operation of stock planning and control procedures. Following the development of appropriate forecasting, and ordering decision rules and procedures, a computer may be used to maintain stock records, initiate purchase or production orders, print out stock-exception reports, status reports, etc.

(3) The design and testing of decision rules. Several computer manufacturers and consultants offer programs for use in designing and testing stock-control procedures. Simulation procedures are usually adopted to develop appropriate methods. In one such system* three sets of information are input to the computer:

(a) Historical transaction data showing the quantities of each item received into and/or issued from stores over a period of time, and showing the dates of each transaction

(b) Stock bin data showing for each item the order lead time, price, set-up costs, etc.

(c) Operating costs data showing costs of holding stock, ordering, etc.

The program can be used to analyse the transaction data, to test several methods of forecasting and a variety of stock ordering rules. Comparison of simulated results using such rules and procedures will enable the system most appropriate to the circumstances to be selected, and will also facilitate comparison of the performance of this system against the performance of the procedures previously used.

Considerable progress has been made recently on the automation of stock and materials handling systems. In 1967 there

* 'Stockplan' by ICL.

were about fifty automated warehouses in the USA and the number of such computer applications is increasing both in that country and in Europe. Developments are also taking place on a somewhat broader front, namely the automation through real time computing of complete materials and parts handling and storage systems. One such computer application is in operation at the Rohr Corporation (USA). The Aircraft Division of the Rohr Corporation was faced with increasing work-in-progress and difficulties in locating parts and tools. Their production control and scheduling was already being handled by a computer, but to help in the storage and control of parts two new real-time systems – AUTOMOVE and RADAR – were devised.

As part of the AUTOMOVE program an automatic warehouse was specially designed and constructed. The warehouse has 16,684 pigeon holes large enough to handle 85 per cent of the parts used at Rohr; further, there are fifteen computer operated stacker cranes and a powered conveyor system.

When a work centre requires more work, the requirement is input to the central computer complex which determines the job with the highest priority for that work centre; it checks that the tools are available, and if not selects the next job. If the parts are stored in the automatic warehouse the computer notifies the local warehouse computer which orders the crane to pull out and dispatch the parts required.

On receipt of parts at the warehouse they are automatically sensed for size and weight, this information together with details of the parts are recorded by the central computer which selects a storage location, and instructs the warehouse computer.

The RADAR (Rohr Automatic Data Acquisition and Retrieval) system also operates real-time. Throughout the plant are 144 specially adapted data phone stations. Anyone wishing to know the location of a part taps out the appropriate information, the computer then searches the locations file and returns the required information in spoken form. This system also permits the immediate updating of status records as parts are moved, and the maintenance of accurate location files.

The Molins company have developed a computer based system

to deal with the handling of materials, tools and parts, as part of their advanced 'System 24' manufacturing system. Working in conjunction with IBM they have developed an automatic conveyor system known as MOLACs (Molins on-line automatic conveyors) which transfer work automatically to and from a storage rack which holds items required by the automated machine tools. The computer ensures that work is provided to operators whose responsibility is to set up materials (pre-drilled billets) on pallets. The MOLAC provides pallets from the storage rack, and delivers the pallets with billets to the storage together with the appropriate tools ready for machining. The system automatically removes these items from the storage rack and delivers them to the appropriate machine tool where they are automatically loaded. Control tapes for the numerically controlled machine tools are also loaded automatically at the computer and on completion of machining a MOLAC replaces the item together with tools in the storage rack, from where it is moved automatically either to the appropriate machine tool for the next operation, or to an operator for further setting prior to the next operation. When all machining operations have been completed the pallet is delivered to the operators ready for unloading. The empty pallets are returned to the storage rack and the finished part is taken automatically to an area before it is sent to another part of the factory.

Molins developed this system together with machine tools in order to cope with the batch-production problems. One of the tremendous benefits of the system is that twenty-four-hour operation is possible with one-shift labour working. Molins claim that the use of this system of batch manufacture leads to reduction in production costs by up to 90 per cent.

MAINTENANCE AND REPAIR

Perhaps the principal use of computers in maintenance is in issuing instructions or orders for both types of maintenance work, i.e. preventive maintenance and repair work. However in this type of application the computer can be called upon to play a far greater part by, for example, scheduling maintenance work, determining the size of maintenance and repair teams, scheduling overtime work, ordering and maintaining a record of spare parts and materials and calculating maintenance and repair costs. Few, if any, computer installations embrace all of these tasks; however there is no reason whatsoever why such a system cannot be designed.

To illustrate the potential scope of computer application in this area we shall describe briefly a 'complete' computerized maintenance system proposed recently by Turban.*

The major parts of the system are shown in Figure 92. The principal part of this, as of any other computer-based system are the master files, containing data for all items of equipment. These files must be regularly updated so as to include valid information on equipment location, age, repairs, cost, maintenance details concerning the maintenance personnel; maintenance tools, spares and materials, etc.

Input to the computer is likely to be largely routine information concerning completed maintenance orders, showing the labour, materials and parts used. The principal output (output 1 – Figure 92) deals with preventive maintenance requirements and provides details of work orders (possibly by craft or skill), materials and spares reservations, etc., time requirements and possibly complete work schedules showing overtime requirements and priorities. Additional output may be required to list complete or delayed jobs to be rescheduled during the next maintenance period.

Such a system would also be used to provide information for maintenance department control and management (output 2 – Figure 92). For this purpose information such as cost comparisons and summaries, materials and spare parts, stock records, and efficiency statements may be required. Such information may also be provided for individual machines (output 3), additionally it may be possible to obtain special reports (output 4) concerning

* E. Turban, 'The Complete Computerized Maintenance System', *Industrial Engineering*, March 1969, pp. 20–27.

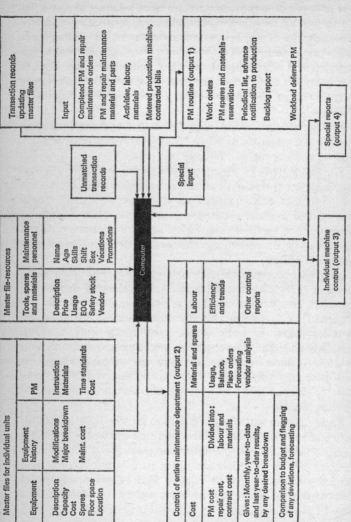

Figure 92 The Major Parts of a Complete Computerized Maintenance System Reproduced with modifications, by permission from E. Turban, 'The Complete Computerized Maintenance System', *Journal of Industrial Engineering*, March 1969, pp. 20–27.

such things as future manpower requirements, preventive/repair cost ratios, failure rates, etc.

Whilst there are yet comparatively few computer installations which cover all of the functions described above and in the figure, the development of such comprehensive systems is proceeding rapidly, and in addition many companies have developed computer-based systems peculiar to their own requirements. For example there are many systems which use computer-based network analysis for the planning and control of maintenance, repair or replacement operations, especially in industries where equipment is complex or large, such as in power stations, aircraft maintenance, etc. Computers may be used in diagnostic procedures to identify faults and determine the extent of maintenance or repair requirements. Occasionally such operations are undertaken automatically, i.e. the computer recognizes the occurrence of a fault or failure, stops the equipment concerned, determines the nature of the failure and calls for appropriate maintenance. This type of continuous automatic monitoring system is used extensively in process control and in industries such as electricity supply, where the consequences of undetected equipment failure are enormous.

QUALITY CONTROL AND INSPECTION

Many of the calculations involved in using the established analytical production management techniques are simple and repetitive, and nowhere more so than in the area of quality assurance and control. Sampling of both attributes and variables, the construction of control limits, and the plotting of control charts are all repetitive procedures capable of being placed under the control of a computer system.

One such system has been developed at the Motorola plant at Phoenix, Arizona where semi-conductors are subject to as many as four tests, the combined results of which are analysed automatically. Figure 93 is a block diagram of the system.

In the United Kingdom, Raleigh Industries has developed a system to automate and improve the inspection of the 250 million machined components produced each year. The system maintains a regular check on machine tool performance in order to detect possible changes in accuracy. Sampled components are placed by the inspectors into special jigs, fitted with electro-magnetic measuring transducers. The inspector presses a test button and the dimensions are signalled, via analog-to-digital converters, to the on-line computer. While the computer carries out its check program a WAIT signal is shown, after which an OK or REJECT signal is given. While the computer signals its decision to each jig operator it also stores the results of the tests in the form of histograms which illustrate the degree to which the inspected dimensions are on or off specification. The computer indicates whether the sample has passed the inspection plan and, on request, prints out the histogram of each dimension. As each part is checked the computer can print out the dimension so that the need to reset the machine tools can be established before rejections have to be made.

The possible shape of things to come is illustrated by the production line for solid logic boards at IBM's Endicott plant, where the central control unit controls the numerical data supplied to the machines on the line. There are also numerically controlled testing machines which send data back to the central unit for interpretation and action.

FURTHER AND FUTURE APPLICATIONS

The type of applications briefly described above are by no means exhaustive; indeed these may be considered to be the more conventional type of application now operating in many companies. In addition to these 'traditional' applications, computers are also used in a wide range of fields related to the production function. For example, at a comparatively simple level, digital computers are used to analyse time-study data, to control assembly lines, to lay out equipment and departments, to calculate incentive

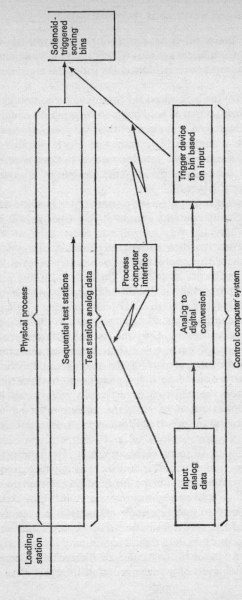

Figure 93 Block Diagram of Motorola Semiconductor Device Inspection and Sorting System

Reprinted by Permission from D. D. Bedworth, 'Discrete Part Manufacturing Control by Digital Computer', *Journal of Industrial Engineering*, Vol. 18, No. 2, 1967.

payments, to synthesize times for operations using synthetic or PMTS data, etc. Computers are also widely used in production technology, for example to control machine tools and machining centres.

As a research tool the high-speed electronic digital computer is invaluable, so much so that it is difficult to imagine how many research workers managed to undertake their work ten or fifteen years ago. Without computers it would be virtually impossible to conduct effective research into the design and performance of priority rules in dispatching or into the design of complex assembly lines (see Chapter 6).

The manner in which computers have been used in business has changed fundamentally over the comparatively brief period of time since their potential was recognized. Early applications derived largely from the then current mechanized office procedures, and consequently involved tasks such as payroll calculations, invoicing, order processing, etc. Such applications still constitute a major proportion of all computer applications; however it is now widely recognized that to obtain maximum benefit from an expensive computer installation applications must range beyond routine data processing. Over the last ten or fifteen years computers have begun to emerge as essential business resources whose use forms an integral part of the managerial function rather than a mere appendage. This change in outlook has derived not only from the increasing expertise of systems analysts, the increasing sophistication of software, increasing machine capacity and speed and the use of random-access stores, but also because of the growing complexity and competitiveness of business and the failure of many early computer installations to provide any commercial benefit. It is now increasingly recognized that computers potentially provide the information skeleton upon which effective managerial procedures may be built. Many companies are attempting to integrate their managerial procedures through the use of the vast information storage capacities and computational speeds of modern digital computers. Increasingly, future applications will see the computer, or hierarchies of computers, pervading all levels of management and thus providing a degree of integration and synergy which has previously been impossible in complex business organizations.

The system flow diagram shown in Figure 87 represented a degree of integration of computer application in the production function, in that the system described embraces production, inventory and purchasing in an attempt to provide a complete materials management system. At present many computer applications in production are confined to specific areas such as stock control, dispatching, etc. However the potential for integration is large: for example, the information obtainable from completed job tickets is not only basic to production control, but essential for accounting (job costing) and payroll (bonus earnings) purposes. Indeed in many respects, the issue of job cards to operators and their return are perhaps the most important information points in the production process, and the adoption of local shop-floor data collection terminals to feed this information to the production-planning and control and accounting systems is clearly an essential prerequisite for effective integrated management control.

Despite the fact that many companies have experienced difficulty in attempting to install so-called integrated management information systems, their peripheral devices to facilitate this integration and coordination of managerial planning and control will undoubtedly be a principal feature of management practice in the near future.

The production function, as it is central to business, will necessarily be a focus of such developments. Furthermore, the increasing sophistication and complexity of production facilities will necessitate the use of refined managerial procedures. The continued development of computer hardware and software will provide the vehicle for such systems, but to be efficient these systems must incorporate effective decision rules and algorithms, which as we have seen throughout this book are currently in short supply, and may remain scarce unless further effort is devoted to production management research.

Apart from their general nature, future applications of the now ubiquitous computer are difficult, perhaps impossible, to predict with any degree of accuracy. Indeed, there is probably only one thing about which we can be reasonably certain: that the computer will find increasing application in industry and commerce, and that in so doing it will affect the lives of all of us to an even greater extent than at present. The computer will surely play a larger part in the planning and control of production in industry in the future, culminating probably in the design of a fully automated, remotely controlled, self-monitoring and -correcting manufacturing facility.

READING REFERENCES

Bedworth, D. D., 'Discrete Part Manufacturing Control by Digital Computer', *Journal of Industrial Engineering*, Vol. XVIII, No. 2, 1967, pp. 159–66, (includes description of Motorola and IBM/Endicott systems).

de Bellow, J., 'Automatic Warehouse Linked to Information Systems', *Industrial Engineering*, Aug. 1969, pp. 14–19 (Rohr 'Automove' and 'Radar' systems).

Blee, M., 'Batch Production via Numerical Control', *Data Systems*, June 1968, pp. 38–55 (Molins system).

Foster, *Automatic Warehousing*, Iliffe, 1970.

Grant, R., 'Jobbing on Line', *Business Management*, July 1969, pp. 31–3 (the Parsons system).

Hall, P. G., 'Engineering and Production Information Control', *Computer Bulletin*, August 1968, pp. 132–43 (the BAC 'EPIC' system).

Smith, R. M., 'Automated Inventory–Production Control', *Management Services*, Sept.–Oct. 1965, pp. 18–25 (the Burroughs system).

Tatham, L., 'The CAV Integrated System', *Data Systems*, Sept. 1967, pp. 33–37 (the CAV system).

CHAPTER 8

The Behavioural Sciences and Production Management

It is fashionable nowadays to examine management problems from a quantitative point of view. This clearly important approach is often referred to as management science, but it should be remembered that mathematics is by no means the only branch of the formal sciences which is important in management. Equally important are economics, sociology, psychology, all of which might be considered as further management sciences.

These latter sciences, which we shall collectively refer to as the behavioural sciences, are of fundamental importance in management since all are concerned with aspects of human behaviour, and all organizations are dependent upon the behaviour of human beings.

If we were to consider the use of science in management in terms of the interest or involvement of specific types of scientist in industry, then we would conclude that the use of the analytical sciences predates the use of the behavioural sciences, because until as little as a hundred years ago engineers dominated industry and management. However this type of argument leads to a considerable underestimation of the use of the behavioural sciences. Whilst early industrialists (and researchers) are characterized by their mechanistic or 'engineering' approach, they were undoubtedly called upon to use behavioural skills since then, as now, management problems were largely concerned with inter-personal and inter-group relations. Indeed, whilst it would be true to say that certain of the behavioural sciences (for example, sociology) have developed only comparatively recently, this does not mean that the fundamental principles of such sciences did not influence managerial behaviour before their incorporation in a formal body of knowledge.

Behavioural problems have been and will remain an important feature of the manager's job for just so long as human beings form an essential part of industry and organizations.

THE GROWTH OF INDUSTRY
AND THE BEHAVIOURAL SCIENCES

Some five thousand years ago men began to live in cities. Folk societies amalgamated to form the first urban communities and for the first time some degree of specialization and division of labour began to develop. Urbanization and occupational specialization was considerably accelerated by the Industrial Revolution which brought about vast improvements in agriculture, manufacture, transportation and communication. Throughout this period new forms of occupational structure began to develop, necessitating a far greater degree of organization or administration.

This process of industrialization has continued unabated to the present day, encouraged – indeed accelerated – by technological, social and political developments. The evolution of an industrialized society was of course accompanied by numerous social problems, many of which still exist today. For example, although the general motives and needs of workers have changed over the past two hundred years from an emphasis on security and sustenance to the dominance of social and self fulfillment needs, such motives remain very much the key to many managerial problems.

Over this period the objectives and the role of business has changed. As little as fifty years ago few people would have suggested that the object of business was anything more than profit maximization, whereas now it is more widely recognized that business and industry have important responsibilities to their employees and to society as a whole.* The recognition of these responsibilities has reinforced the role of the behavioural sciences in industry, and as a result there is now widespread interest in the need to ensure job satisfaction for employees, the provision of adequate training and individual development and so on.

*For example only recently has industry's responsibility to society for aspects of the physical environment been recognized as a result of international concern with problems of pollution and conservation.

Numerous other developments during this period have had the effect of radically changing both the role of business in relation to society and consumer, and the relationships of employees to their jobs and employers. The emergence of a population of relatively affluent and discerning consumers has affected the marketing, promotional and production policies of companies and accelerated the evolution of economics as a business discipline. The unionization of labour has radically affected the personnel function and given rise to the industrial relations function in business, a now traditional domain of the behavioural scientist. During the first and second world wars the pressure to increase productivity encouraged the investigation by psychologists of the problems of fatigue and monotony, and the later development of ergonomics added momentum to such research.

More recently industrial expansion accompanied by high employment opportunities and comparatively low unemployment rates has encouraged the investigation by behavioural scientists of problems such as labour turnover and absenteeism, whilst the increasing use of automated procedures and computers has encouraged a series of investigations concerning their effects on employees.

The Industrial Training Act has encouraged investment in training at all levels, particularly operator training, again requiring the specialist knowledge of the behavioural or social scientist.

Perhaps the most important contribution of behavioural scientists to research in management derived from the famous experiments begun at the Hawthorne works of the American Western Electric Company in the early 1920s. The results of these investigations did much to modify the scientific management theories of management developed earlier (largely by engineers such as Taylor), by promoting an awareness of the importance of the social work group. These investigations sparked off many further investigations some of which have had important effects on current management thinking. In the early decades of this century many theories of management or organization were developed, such as Scientific Management which emphasized the mechanistic, engineering approach; Human Relations theory which emphasized the importance of social relations, and Human Resources theory which emphasized the importance of workers' abilities and achievement needs. A great deal was learnt during this period, but in many respects these theories can be likened to a blind man's view of an elephant in that they represent an incomplete, and above all inadequate, picture of the situation. Much of this early work is now considered as somewhat naïve in its simplicity and it is increasingly recognized that the complexities of many industrial organization or managerial problems are far greater than had hitherto been realized. Few if any general behavioural principles or rules have been developed to assist the manager, who must therefore rely upon his knowledge of current thinking in this area in order to be able to synthesize what appear to him to be satisfactory strategies for the problems at hand. This applies no less to the production function than to any other aspect of business.

BEHAVIOURAL PROBLEMS AND PRODUCTION MANAGEMENT

Few if any production procedures operate without the assistance or support of human manual work; indeed such workers are the principal resources of most industries. The behaviour of these workers during their hours of employment is an important determinant of industrial efficiency, and the task of studying their behaviour falls largely to the behavioural scientist. The implications of such studies are evident in every aspect of production management; consequently, the discussion below must of necessity form only an abbreviated examination of certain aspects of the subject.

Location, Layout and Arrangements of Facilities

The selection of a suitable location for a plant is more than a mere logistics problem, especially in labour-intensive industries. In the UK the choice of location will be influenced by government legislation and incentives, which under present policy encourage companies to establish facilities in one of several development areas. In selecting a location a company must normally consider the nature and extent of the available labour-force, in particular its skills, traditions and culture.

Important characteristics are discernible in various parts of the country. For example, mining areas are known to suffer from high absenteeism. Furthermore, and at a more basic level, research has tended to indicate that cultural and community factors are related to intelligence, aspirations, and, to a lesser extent, personality. For example, many investigations in this country and elsewhere have demonstrated that urban children tend to have both higher intelligence levels and higher educational and occupational aspirations than equivalent rural children. Recent research in America, and to a lesser extent in the U K, has shown that community factors such as urban/rural differences are related to job attitudes, in that workers in urban areas are apparently more tolerant of and satisfied in rationalized repetitive jobs than rural workers. Rural workers have been found to be more satisfied with their wage levels than equivalent urban workers, and it is also suggested that social needs and attitudes to social work-group relations differ between urban and rural workers.

These findings, together with the more obvious regional differences, have important but frequently ignored implications for management. It is conceivable that with the increasing awareness of the importance of human factors in industry, coupled with the need for companies to take all possible steps to avoid expensive problems such as industrial disputes or labour turnover and absenteeism, such factors may in future play a greater part in locational decision-making.

From discussions in earlier chapters it is clear that certain types of plant layout are fundamentally more appropriate to certain types of production. However, consideration of material and parts flow and handling costs should not be allowed to obscure the human implications of the various types of facilities layout. Layout by product, for example, normally necessitates the use of semi- or unskilled workers, who are often subjected to quite

considerable pressures by way of imposed patterns of work behaviour, e.g. short-cycle work, with closely defined work methods
and very close 'pacing'. Furthermore, in this type of layout freedom of movement is often severely limited not only because of
the nature of the work but also because of the arrangement of the
facilities. In comparison, layout by process depends often upon
the use of skilled operatives working independently. In this type
of layout freedom of movement is very much greater, and in
addition this type of arrangement lends itself to the provision of
specialized supervision.

Clearly there is a conflict between, on one hand, the need to
rationalize operations and increase production volume in order to
achieve the efficiency associated with mass production, and on
the other hand, the need to retain work and production groups
which are small enough to facilitate communication and identifi-
cation. The problem therefore is to what extent technological and
engineering considerations are to be permitted to structure production arrangements which are considered behaviourally un-
satisfactory. Clearly the production arrangement to be adopted
should be the one which provides minimum total cost operation.
Unfortunately, however, the direct cost benefits associated with
technological and engineering factors are frequently easier to
identify and measure than the indirect cost considerations associated with behaviour factors such as labour turnover, absenteeism, output restriction and disputes, and consequently in
practice it has often proved very difficult to identify the compromise which leads to minimum total cost operation. Indeed,
because of such difficulties and in the absence of clear unequivocal
behavioural principles the indirect cost consequences of such
decisions have often been ignored. Because of the uniqueness of
all such situations general solutions are impossible, and each case
can only be treated on its own merit. From time to time certain
'solutions' to our methods of overcoming such problems become
fashionable and companies adopt them, often with success. However, it would be unwise to suppose that within the conceivable
future any panacea will be discovered.

'Cell-type' production offers one method of satisfying, in part, the conflicting demands of technological and behavioural requirements in facilities layout. This type of production offers a compromise situation in which a large production unit is subdivided into a series of production departments or cells, each responsible for the manufacture of certain items or parts. Within each of these cells one might find a wide range of production processes, arranged in a manner governed by the production requirements of the particular product, but nevertheless the whole is sufficiently small to retain a common identity and interest. Group technology is a similar method of production, since in this system facilities are arranged specifically for the manufacture in large quantities of similar component *parts* rather than products, and so the direct cost benefits of large scale production are often available in situations where a variety of products are made; furthermore the facilities may be arranged in order to obtain some of the benefits associated with small production units.

The task of facilities layout also embraces the problems of work place design. It will be recalled that the Gilbreths, the pioneers of method study, paid considerable attention to the physiological problems of work design (Chapter 6), and as a result were able to develop their 'principles of motion economy' which have influenced both work method design and workplace layout for about half a century. Not only was the development of these principles the first step towards the establishment of general principles of job design, but they were also the forerunners of a whole field of study concerned with the relation of the worker to his working environment, the use of his body and so forth. This field, known as ergonomics in this country and variously as human engineering and human factors engineering elsewhere, gained considerable momentum during the second world war and has retained the interests of psychologists and others ever since.

The design of controls, displays and the physical environment is clearly of considerable importance to the production manager. In certain respects research work in the field of ergonomics has now reached a point which is well beyond the immediate interests of the production manager especially since there is adequate evidence to indicate that ergonomic factors, and especially environmental conditions, are now frequently less important than factors such as payment systems, work content and methods and social relations in determining job satisfaction and behaviour. Classical ergonomic research was concerned with (1)

Task condition	Type of task or area	Illumination level (ft-c)	Type of illumination
Small detail, low brightness contrast, prolonged periods, high speed, extreme accuracy	Sewing, inspecting dark materials, etc.	100	General plus supplementary (e.g., desk lamp)
Small detail, fair contrast, speed not essential	Machining detail drafting, watch repairing, inspecting medium materials, etc.	50–100	General plus supplementary
Normal detail, prolonged periods	Reading, parts assembly, general office and laboratory work	20–50	General (e.g., overhead ceiling fixture)
Normal detail, no prolonged periods	Washrooms, power plants, waiting rooms, kitchens	10–20	General (e.g., random natural or artificial light)
Good contrast, fairly large objects	Recreational facilities	5–10	General
Large objects	Restaurants, stairways, bulk-supply warehouses	2–5	General

Figure 94 Levels of Illumination and Types of Illumination Recommended for Various Task Conditions

Reproduced by permission from A. Chapanis, *Man–Machine Engineering*, Tavistock, 1968.

the design of information displays, (2) the design of controls and (3) environmental factors, and from this research has come a whole series of design standards or recommendations such as the one given in Figure 94 which the industrial engineer may use to assist him in method design and workplace layout.

Work Methods and Job Design

The conflicting principles of industrial engineers and behavioural scientists is nowhere more evident than in the area of work design. Traditional work study practice can be criticized on two counts, firstly unjustified assumptions, and secondly subjective procedures. In method design it is assumed, for example, that there exists a single best method of performing a particular task, and in work measurement it is normally assumed that there is a single correct time for performing a task. Both of these assumptions are clearly and indisputably invalid. To take rather obvious examples, the 'best' method of performing a task (say the quickest) will surely depend upon whether a person is left- or right-handed, whilst the 'correct' time for performing a task (say the quickest time consistent with continuous repetition for several hours) may depend upon the individual's physiological and motor abilities. Having made this criticism it is only fair to say that there is little that the industrial engineer can do to compensate for the inadequacy of these assumptions. Because he cannot reasonably treat each worker as an individual (i.e. redesign each job and establish a new work standard every time a change of operator takes place), he must work from the concept of the *average* operator. Furthermore, because of the second weakness of work study – the subjectivity of the approach – industrial engineers cannot guarantee that the work methods and standards that they establish will necessarily be ideal for the average operator. In other words, for no reason other than circumstance traditional work design is an inexact science. There is little that can be done about this situation; indeed behavioural scientists would argue that little needs to be done since work study should only be considered as the first step in work design.

A great deal of research work has now been conducted in the field of work design, the results of which firmly establish the importance of behavioural scientists in this area. Perhaps the major topic of research has concerned the effects of work pacing and work method enforcement. For example, it has been found that in general operators working efficiently tend to change their work methods from time to time without detriment to their performance; it has been found that the operation time of workers both differ and vary, i.e. that some workers not surprisingly are able to perform tasks more quickly than others and that the operation time of any one individual varies about a mean; it has been found that workers who are unpaced (i.e. do not have to perform each and every operation or cycle in a specific time) tend to have a higher productivity than those who are paced, other things being equal.

The implications of such findings for work-system design are perhaps best illustrated by reference to the design of assembly lines. In Chapter 6 we referred to the problem of assembly-line balancing. The techniques described for line balancing made use of work-measurement data, namely the standard time for work elements, and took as their objective the allocation of work elements to stations so that the sum of element standard times should be the same for each station. A perfectly balanced line, therefore, is a fictional state since we know that element and operation times not only differ but vary. Therefore no assembly line will be perfectly balanced at any time, and the degree of balance will vary continually. Because of the inevitable variation in operation times at manned stations on assembly lines, work pacing (the enforcement of a given cycle time) necessarily produces inefficiencies. Idle time may occur at stations or alternatively work may need to be passed to the next station incomplete. This inefficiency is known as system loss, and as we have mentioned previously workers operating under paced conditions are normally less efficient than those working without pacing.

Again it would seem that the techniques available to the industrial engineer are in themselves inadequate and consequently they should be treated as a necessary yet insufficient part of assembly-line design, since behavioural problems related to the pacing effect necessitate further consideration.

Assembly-line work can also be used to illustrate another problem area, where the skills of behavioural scientists are invaluable to management. Ever since the birth of the scientific management movement the rationalization or specialization of manual work has been a continuing policy in industry. Undoubtedly this work rationalization has led to considerable improvements in productivity and has many advantages with regard to the minimization of training requirements and the transferability of labour. However, it has been suggested recently that this policy may well have reached the point of diminishing returns. The direct cost benefits associated with increased output through continued work rationalization may well be more than offset by the indirect cost detriments of increased labour turnover and absenteeism. Behavioural scientists argue that the continuing trend of work rationalization has run against the trend towards increasing educational levels, that financial and security needs are no longer paramount amongst the majority of the work-force, and that an increasing proportion of manual workers are motivated by achievement and recognition needs and consequently seek more interesting, challenging and varied work. Arguments such as these, supported by empirical research, have led to the establishment of what might be called a job enlargement or enrichment movement, which advocates the redesign of rationalized manual jobs so as to provide more variety and challenge, and more opportunity for the individual to exercise his intellectual abilities.

Faced with high labour turnover and similar behavioural problems, many firms have been encouraged to enlarge or enrich certain manual jobs. Many such job enlargement or enrichment exercises have been conducted, which have produced operating benefits such as increased output, reduced labour turnover and absenteeism and improved quality. For example Conant and Kilbridge* have reported one such exercise, in which conventional assembly lines were replaced by independent work stations. The product being assembled was a washing-machine pump consisting of twenty-seven parts. Assembly was originally undertaken by six men working on a line, each having six elements of work to perform in a cycle time of 0·30 minutes. The enlarged jobs each

* Conant, E. H., Kilbridge, M. D., *Industrial and Labour Relations Review*, Vol. 18, No. 3, 1965, pp. 377–95.

consisted of thirty-five work elements with a cycle time of 1·49 minutes. There was no work pacing and each man was responsible for the quality of his output. This redesign of the work resulted in a reduction in the defective output rate from 2·9 to 1·4 per cent, together with an increase in the productive labour time.

Many such exercises have been reported in learned journals during the last fifteen or twenty years and a great deal has been written and said about the benefits of job enlargement. However the fact that many such exercises have been conducted without beneficial results has tended to be overlooked. In general more success has been achieved from the enlargement of 'white-collar' jobs than from the enlargement of the jobs of manual workers, where the verdict must remain one of 'not proven'.

Notice that job enlargement may be achieved through changes in aspects of the job other than the nature of the work. Such things as payment systems, supervisory arrangements, and inspection procedures may be changed in order to provide the operator with more decision-making opportunities. The problem of job design is therefore somewhat larger than the problem of work design.

We cannot assume that a job which provides satisfaction and/or maximizes productivity for one worker will necessarily have the same effect on his neighbour, since individuals differ not only in their work skills but also in their job needs and attitudes. The problems of work and job design can therefore be considered as similar to the problem facing the tailor who must either measure his customer and make a suit specifically to his requirements, or attempt to make a series of 'off the peg' suits which will provide an adequate fit for the majority of customers. Either way a thorough knowledge of customer 'dimensions' is required, and likewise for the problems of work and job design where dimensions such as abilities, needs and expectations are important. In this context the tasks of deciding what and how to measure fall to the behavioural scientists and the use of such 'measurements' in the design of jobs is the joint responsibility of the industrial engineer and the behavioural scientist. Ideally, of course, one would wish to design each job according to the requirements of the individual workers, but at present this is impossible both for practical reasons and because of a lack of theoretical knowledge. The solution must therefore depend upon providing a variety of jobs (in much the same way as a multiple tailor provides a series of suit sizes) consistent with the needs of most workers. Selection of workers for, and their placement in, such jobs also requires a level of knowledge which is lacking at the present time, and so it must be expected that personnel managers will make mistakes, and that workers will become dissatisfied with the jobs on which they are engaged. For this reason production and personnel managers and their behavioural advisers must institute procedures for identifying dissatisfied workers and providing internal transfers and/or selective job redesign if necessary.

It will be evident from this brief discussion that the problems of job design are interdisciplinary or interdepartmental, both production and personnel departments having responsibilities in the area (Figure 95).

Finally it is worth remembering that these two departments also overlap with respect to training. It is normal for operator training to be the responsibility of the personnel function, but of course training requirements are determined not only by the skills and abilities of the workers selected by the personnel department, but also by the nature of the jobs designed by the industrial engineering or production departments. Behavioural scientists have been concerned with the problems of training for some considerable time, but of late there has been a considerable regeneration of interest in this topic in the UK because of the formation and influence of the Industry Training Boards. The essential features of effective training have been established for some time (see Figure 96), but their implications are sometimes overlooked in the production function. How often, for example, is adequate allowance made for the learning effect and in particular the differing learning curves of different people in work design and in the design of work systems such as assembly lines?

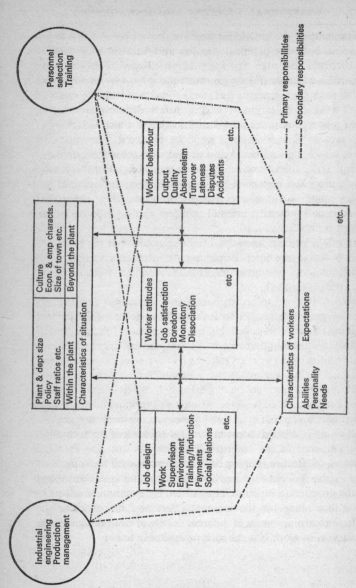

Figure 95 The Nature of and Responsibilities for Job Design

The essentials or principles of training

(1) *The principle of feedback* (or the principle of 'knowledge of results') If results are presented immediately to a trainee subsequent performance is improved. The quicker the feedback of information or performance the more effective the correlation.

(2) *The 'Learning Curve'*

The time required to perform a repetitive task diminishes at first rapidly then more slowly until a constant figure is reached.
In general the following formula applies:

$$T_s = T_1 \left(M + \frac{1 - M}{{}_s m} \right)$$

where T_1 = Time required for first cycle
T_s = Time required for sth cycle
m = Exponent of the reduction in time
M = Factor of incompressibility

Consideration of the 'learning curve' effect is necessary for the adjustment of work schedules, wage rates and work standards.

(3) *Analyse and break down task into components*

i.e. analyse into detail the skills of the trained operator; provide preliminary training exercises in difficult elements; build up into complete performance after mastery of parts.

Figure 96 The Essentials or Principles of Training

(Derived from O. G. Edholm, *The Biology of Work*, World University Library, 1967.)

Quality Control

The well-established analytical methods of quality assurance and control have been described in Chapter 5. Such methods, which were amongst the first applications of mathematics in business, are invaluable in quality control and are used universally. However, as one might have suspected, there is a good deal more to effective quality assurance and control beyond the application of statistical sampling theory. In discussing acceptance sampling it was demonstrated that complete absence of defects could only be ensured through hundred per cent or exhaustive sampling. However it should of course be remembered that even exhaustive sampling cannot be guaranteed to eliminate all defective items unless the inspection processes adopted are perfect, i.e. unless the human inspectors make no mistakes. In other words the quality of the actual inspection process is an important factor underlying the efficiency of statistical quality control and assurance procedures.

We cannot expect any human inspection process to be perfect, since very often the inspection task is repetitive and monotonous, and such conditions are hardly conducive to vigilance. One further source of error is the need for judgement in inspection. In acceptance sampling by variables inspectors are required to examine a certain dimension of an object, and this they frequently achieve by use of gauges of the 'GO/NO-GO' type; however, in acceptance sampling by attributes they are often required to make far less precise judgements. They may, for example, have to decide whether or not to reject an item on the basis of its surface finish, and whilst instruments are available for measuring such characteristics, their use is a good deal less easy than using a caliper gauge. Even more difficult is the assessment of characteristics such as colour, odour and taste and in such cases decisions can only be taken by comparing the item in question to an established standard. Of course this process of comparison is fundamentally the same as comparing a dimension to a given standard, as defined by a gauge, but the amount of judgement required in the two cases differs considerably because of the 'remoteness' of the standard in the former cases. To facilitate this type of judgement the requisite standard should be placed as close as conveniently possible to the place of observation (e.g. the colour chart should be suspended over the work); in certain cases, however, the standard does not exist as a physical entity and in such cases one must rely upon adequate training and regular recalibration of the 'conceptual' or 'mental' standard. In the case of the caliper gauge recalibration may involve adjustment using special measuring equipment, but in the case of standards such as those for colour, taste or odour recalibration may involve some degree of retraining or reinforcement in order to retain the accuracy of a 'mental' standard.

The difficulties associated with inspection processes of this type necessitate special training programmes which emphasize the acquisition of skills in judgement and the demonstration of vigilance. The learning of such skills and training of this type has engaged the attention of psychologists for many years, especially since such training requirements are also a part of other jobs in the military and strategic field. A great deal of relevant work has been undertaken in such topics as learning and control theory, and a large amount of empirical and theoretical knowledge is now available.

Because of the difficulty of many inspectors' tasks environmental conditions are especially important, and in this area a great deal of research work has been undertaken in recent years, again encouraged by the needs of the military. Industrial standards have been developed to cover requirements such as lighting intensity and glare, and other ergonomic factors are of the utmost importance. For example, the arrangement of the items to be inspected into a logical pattern or layout may facilitate inspection by converting the task into one of pattern recognition. The positioning of light sources so as to emphasize the characteristic being inspected (e.g. emphasizing surface irregularities by means of shadows). Mechanical or visual aids may be used, such as templates, scanning devices, masks, comparitors. Attention should be given to the duration of work periods, since it has been found by research workers that vigilance tends to decrease with the increasing time spent on inspection, and also depends to some extent upon the arrangement and duration of work and rest periods. Various factors in the design of inspection tasks are known to affect the efficiency of inspection. For example, the complexity of the inspection task has an effect on inspection performance, better performance being associated with lower complexity (Figure 97). The defect rate (i.e. the percentage of defects produced by the process) has been found to be related to inspection performance, inspection accuracy usually decreasing with a decrease in defect rate (Figure 98). This of course raises the question as to whether inspections should be carried out in the same manner irrespective of the process defective rate.

The social position of the inspector is also worth considering, since this may act as an important influence on his performance.

The inspector occupies a difficult position, since it is his explicit task to 'pass judgement' on the operators amongst whom he is working. This social pressure which derives from such a situation together with the inspector's familiarity with his task and

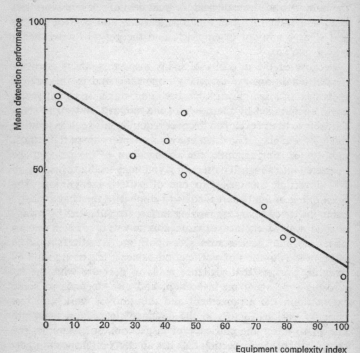

Figure 97 Reproduced by permission from D. H. Harris, F. B. Chaney, *Human Factors in Quality Assurance*, Wiley, 1969.

especially his knowledge of past quality performance may lead to the operation or even the adoption of standards which differ from those originally specified for the process. Because of such possibilities it is perhaps advisable to consider some form of job rotation for inspection workers or even the use of quality checks on their work. It has been suggested that inspectors should be organized into groups and allowed to develop their own standards. The even more far-reaching suggestion has been made that in many cases traditional inspection procedures should be discarded, and responsibility for quality given to the operator.

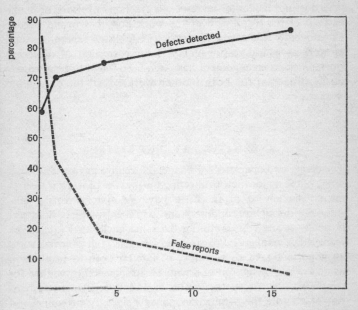

Figure 98 Reproduced by permission from D. H. Harris, F. B. Chaney, *Human Factors in Quality Assurance,* Wiley, 1969.

Indeed this is often the result of job enlargement or enrichment exercises, where the object is to increase the content, challenge and responsibility of jobs. Whether responsibility for quality is vested in the inspector or not, the need for feedback to the operator is essential. In fact this feedback of performance, information or knowledge of results is one important behavioural principle. It is argued and has been demonstrated that very often such knowledge provides motivation at work and is essential for effective training. Few behavioural scientists would therefore dispute the need for inspectors to return or at least notify operators of quality defects, yet in practice such a procedure is often absent. For example, the conventional design of assembly lines does not facilitate the return, correction or rework of items because of the disruption of the work flow that would occur. Consequently it is often necessary to establish a separate group of workers whose responsibility is for correction of defective work. Such an arrangement has often been found to be a source of dissatisfaction for both the line workers and the correction workers.

INCENTIVE PAYMENT SYSTEMS

The design and operation of financial incentive payment systems is one of the major factors affecting the practice of work measurement. The nature of incentive payment systems varies substantially throughout industry and whilst this subject does not normally succeed in capturing the same intellectual interest as many other managerial/organizational subjects, it is nevertheless an important area of research, of interest both to production managers and behavioural scientists. Responsibility neither for the design nor for the operation of incentive payment systems rests solely with the production manager since the personnel and industrial relations functions are heavily involved. However, the production function is closely concerned with the subject since the production manager is usually responsible for providing data (work standards) and subsequently for the implementation and operation of such schemes. (The problems stemming from this source often occupy a considerable proportion of the production manager's time.) In spite of the large amounts of money spent and the obvious relevance of behavioural theory for industrial compensation practices there is probably less solid research in this area than in any other field related to worker performance. The importance of motivation in determining worker behaviour has been pointed out elsewhere in this chapter, and again in the present context the nature of worker motivation is of primary importance. The role of monetary rewards in relation to worker motivation has been discussed by many writers. Money has been described as an 'anxiety reducer', as a 'conditioned reinforcer', a 'condition incentive' and, more recently as a 'hygiene factor' capable of causing job dissatisfaction if not present in adequate amounts but incapable of providing job satisfaction.

Research in this area has dealt with the relation of financial compensation to the characteristics of the job and to the personal characteristics of job holders. It has been found that the 'schedule' of payment, i.e. the manner in which payment levels are determined and the degree of secrecy surrounding payment, have important effects on workers' attitudes to their wages. There is considerable evidence to suggest that normally the installation of incentive payment plans results in greater output per man-hour, lower unit costs and higher wages in comparison with results associated with straight (or 'flat') payment systems.

Incentive plans are geared to either the worker's own output or the total output of his working group and studies have shown that individual output decreases as the size of the work group increases, a feature which is apparently due to workers' perceiving a decreased probability that their efforts will yield increased production.

Financial incentives frequently do not lead to increased output, and group standards and social pressures often induce workers to perform considerably below their potential levels. The secrecy surrounding the amount of money given an employee may have motivational implications; recent studies indicate that secret pay policies may contribute to dissatisfaction with pay and lead to the possibility of lowered job performance.

The effectiveness of incentive plans in general appears to depend upon the worker's knowledge of the relation between performance and earnings. (In one study, only 38 per cent of the workers perceived increased performance as leading to increased earnings, whilst 35 per cent of the work force perceived low productivity as an aid to higher earnings in the long run.)

Some research workers report that piece-rate systems lead to fewer symptoms of boredom than do straight hourly payment systems. However, even if piece-work systems relieve boredom, output under such plans may still suffer if the task being performed is disliked by the workers. Indeed the general concensus of studies is that repetitive, destructive, boring or disliked tasks are apparently much less susceptible to monetary incentives.

The perceived importance of pay to workers is clearly an important factor in the design of any rewards system, yet unfortunately little useful generalization is possible concerning the relative importance of the financial need. Many contemporary studies have shown that the need for adequate wages is of paramount importance whilst others have tended to place this need below that of achievement, affiliation needs, and so on. Clearly the importance of the financial need is closely related to the specific circumstances surrounding an individual. For example, a person living and working in an area offering comparatively few alternative employment opportunities may place somewhat more importance on the financial need than say, a female, unmarried, part-time worker living and working in a large city where alternative employment opportunities abound. The difficulty of attempting to estimate the importance of monetary rewards to workers, and perhaps the false basis of many financial incentive payment systems, was illustrated by the results of a piece of research in which employees were asked to rank eight factors including pay in order of importance. The employees ranked pay in third position; however their employers, when asked to rank these factors according to how they thought the employees would respond, selected pay as the most important factor.

There is a wide variety of types of incentive payment system in operation in industry at the moment, and as in many other managerial problem areas the difficulty now lies not in devising more systems, but in devising procedures to assist in selecting one or more of the available systems for use in specific circumstances. Recent research in this area, reflecting the general trend of behavioural research, has moved towards the examination of the wider, multivariate nature of this problem. Lupton, for example, is studying the relation of incentive payment systems to such factors as the nature of the local labour market, the nature of production, turnover and absenteeism as well as the characteristics of the job. He has attempted to classify methods of incentive payment according to the nature of the motivational principle upon which they are based, and the type of effort or attribute that they are designed to regard (Figure 99).

			Reward principle		
			Reciprocal		Non-Reciprocal
			Immediate	Deferred	
Type of effort rewarded		Time	Time rates, with reciprocal payments e.g. shift and overtime premiums	Time rates, with reciprocal payments (or their equivalents) deferred, e.g. day off in lieu	Pay hour by hour for the hour
	Energy	Individual	Piecework Incentive bonus schemes Simple multi-factor schemes	Individual productivity bonus Personal contract schemes	Task work Measured day work Controlled day work
		Group	Group piecework Group Incentive bonus schemes Group simple multi-factor schemes Price lists	Group productivity bonus Scanlon and Rucker type schemes Profit sharing	Contract work
		Competence	Complex multi-factor schemes Analytical estimating	Work simplification Incremental scales with 'bars' based on performance	Full incremental salary scales Professional fees

Figure 99 Classification of Incentive Payment Systems

Based on T. Lupton, 'Decision Theory and Human Relations in Industry', *The Production Engineer*, Vol. 48, No. 11, Nov. 1969, pp. 487–98.

The problems associated with the design, selection, installation, implementation and operation of incentive payment systems are complex and as in many of the other areas that we have discussed such problems, because of their association with the needs, attitudes and behaviour of individuals are not susceptible to general solutions.

AN EXAMPLE OF THE INFLUENCE OF 'BEHAVIOURAL' THINKING IN PRODUCTION MANAGEMENT

Production management, like any other aspect of management, possesses its own techniques and procedures, some long-established and universally adopted, others fashionable but transient. From time to time there comes on the scene a new technique or procedure which pervades the technical press and is eventually digested, or dismissed by practitioners, or seized upon by consultants and academics and used in the development of improved or more comprehensive techniques. Value Analysis, Group Technology and Network Analysis are examples of techniques which have found a permanent and useful place and Zero Defects is an example of a technique currently 'under offer'. Developed in America by the Martin Company of Florida, this technique, which has been used with considerable success by many companies, may be categorized as a 'production man's behavioural procedure for quality assurance' or, in the words of the originators, as 'a new dimension in quality assurance'.

Many of the applications or implications of the behavioural sciences which were discussed earlier in this chapter derived from the application of established psychological, sociological and economic principles, or from deliberate research in the field of production. In contrast zero defects is behavioural pragmatism and is worth studying briefly not only for its own merit as a production management technique, but also as a possible signpost to future developments.

Zero defects is basically an employee motivational programme designed to encourage error-free performance by appealing to the individual employee's pride of workmanship. It is argued that workers often adopt 'double standards' in demanding perfection from the people that serve them, such as the shopkeeper, dentist and doctor, without giving the same performance themselves, and since work errors do not affect them personally, workers give less than their best performance and maintain that 'management expects some mistakes'. To reverse this situation, it is argued, this state of 'conditioning' must be dismissed and employees must be encouraged to take a personal interest and pride in their work, in much the same way as they expect their dentist to take pride (and care) whilst extracting their teeth. Defects or worker errors can be caused by (1) lack of knowledge, (2) lack of proper facilities and (3) lack of care and attention; zero defects is concerned with the latter.

The zero defect concept is intended to promote a conscious desire in a worker to do any job right first time, to promote constant awareness that his task is important. In this respect ZD (as it is often called by followers) is not claimed to be original in concept, but merely the application of fundamental behavioural principles in an original manner.

The basic steps necessary to establish ZD are given in Figure 100. Clearly there is nothing startlingly new about this technique. There are no original principles or formulae, and it is only the use and presentation of these principles that is in any way original. The technique attempts to release the one basic quality resource, namely individual care and skill, and in doing so utilizes sound behavioural thinking plus a liberal dressing of salesmanship. For example a common feature of ZD programmes is the ZD pledge signed by workers. (E.g. 'I freely pledge myself constantly to strive for improved quality of workmanship and will be ever conscious that I am an important part in each of our successes.') Posters, displays and exhibitions play an important part in promoting quality awareness. Seminars are often held to discuss 'error cause removal' policies, suggestion schemes are used; recognition certificates and awards are presented publicly to employees and suppliers and the unions are encouraged to establish their own reward system. Group quality performances are

(1) Management committee :
   obtain complete and positive executive backing for programme

(2) Establish a Quality Improvement Team

(3) Establish methods of measuring quality performance

(4) Establish methods of determining quality and defective costs

(5) Promote quality awareness :
   to prepare for ZD

(6) Establish defective prevention systems

(7) Training programmes

(8) Launch ZD to all personnel :
   obtain commitment from all personnel

(9) Goal setting :
   turn commitments into action by getting personnel to establish improvement goals for themselves

(10) Error cause removal :
   i.e. establish procedure for recording causes of errors and removal of such causes

(11) Recognition :
   i.e. to provide recognition and rewards to employees who make greatest contribution to improved quality

(12) Quality council :
   to provide a method of guiding and developing quality management in the firm

Figure 100 Steps in a ZD Programme

displayed in prominent places, pin-badges are awarded and promotional meetings and rallies held. Workers are encouraged to meet customers and suppliers and above all the ZD programme is advanced as a cooperative effort, an 'across the board' programme relying on worker–management cooperation and individual effort.

The use of this type of technique may seem somewhat unusual to British eyes but it is quite common in North America. It is very easy for those of us who are unused to this type of approach to dismiss techniques such as ZD as gimmicks, and indeed it is difficult to imagine many companies in this country enthusiastically adopting such a technique and applying it with the showmanship and fervour practised and advocated in its country of origin. The fact that it is somewhat out of step with current practice should not, however, mean its dismissal, since it is both soundly based and of proved merit in certain industries. It will be seen, for example, that it has behavioural foundations that are both intuitively and empirically sound. The technique recognizes the importance of worker motivation in the determination of performance levels, and provides for the fulfilment of achievement, recognition and affiliation needs. The principles of feedback of results, reward, and positive reinforcement of performance are included, as also are facilities for individual and group establishment of targets and standards. The technique attempts to release the individual abilities and efforts of workers in much the same manner as job enlargement. Looked at in another way, it attempts to lead an organization and its workers to better productivity rather than to push them towards that goal. In this respect it differs from any other industrial engineering techniques whose purpose may be seen as inducement (e.g. work pacing and incentive payments).

This example raises an interesting topic for discussion. We have seen throughout this chapter that whilst the behavioural sciences have a great deal to contribute to production management, there are few areas in which answers or principles are available. Rather, in most instances, it is a case of being aware of the implications and attempting from the incomplete theoretical and empirical knowledge available, to synthesize adequate strategies, or at least to apply conventional techniques with the full knowledge of their limitations. Furthermore, we have seen throughout this book that there are few rigorous analytical techniques which are of demonstrable value to production management. In such circumstances a production manager must use his judgement and familiarity with the present inadequate body of knowledge in devising techniques and procedures appropriate to his own circumstances. Zero defects and similar techniques are of course designed for precisely this type of situation, and we cannot afford to ignore them solely because they are intellectually unattractive or somewhat lacking in their empirical pedigrees. How much better is it for example to utilize a technique such as zero defects to provide a ten or twenty per cent improvement in quality, than to devote excess energies to obtaining marginal improvements in quality performance through the use of refined modifications to statistical sampling procedures?

Nor of course are the merits of the ZD-type approach confined to the problems of quality assurance. There is no reason whatsoever why a similar technique cannot be devised to assist in production control – *quantity assurance*, perhaps. The fundamental objectives of ZD are quite simple and there is no reason why such a behavioural approach should not be used to release motivational forces to the benefit of other aspects of production.

READING REFERENCES

Brown, J. A. C., *The Social Psychology of Industry*, Penguin, 1954.

Harris, D. H., Chaney, F. B., *Human Factors in Quality Assurance*, Wiley, 1969.

Harpin, J. F., *Zero Defects*, McGraw-Hill, 1966.

Marriott, R., *Incentive Payment Systems*, Staples Press, 1968.

Murrell, K. F. H., *Ergonomics*, Prentice Hall, 1965.

Wild, R., Hill, A. B., *Women in the Factory*, Inst. of Personnel Managers, 1970.

CHAPTER 9

Production Management – Problems and Perspectives

PRODUCTION occupies a fairy-tale position in both industry and education, but unfortunately the role played is that of Cinderella rather than Prince Charming. Few people would seriously dispute the importance of the production function in business but this importance is frequently unrelated to the importance attached to it in the board-room, and is certainly not reflected in the importance attached to the subject in educational circles.

Production engineering has only comparatively recently evolved in this country as a profession and as a respectable educational subject, and production management has yet to evolve at all, in either context. Thanks mainly to the efforts of the professional body and certain enlightened educational establishments, production engineering as a subject is now moving from strength to strength and tremendous advances are being made, many of which are having or are destined to have far reaching effects in industry. In the past ten or so years production processes such as electro-chemical machining, spark erosion, high-rate forming, powder metallurgy, electron-beam welding and investment casting have been developed. New production concepts such as numerical control, automated assembly and inspection, group technology, cell manufacture and modular production have evolved and new technologies such as solid-state electronics, cryogenics, ultrasonics and tribology have helped in the transformation of production practice. During this time the complexity and cost of production equipment has increased and a widening gulf has become evident between the capabilities of production processes and management's abilities to utilize such processes and equipment in an efficient manner. In other words there is evidence that

* Based partly on R. Wild, 'Production: Current Prospectives for Management Education', *Management Education and Development*, Vol. 2, No. 1, 1971.

production management knowledge and ability is growing more slowly than production engineering knowledge and ability.

Furthermore it should be remembered that the external pressures influencing industry have changed considerably over the past ten years. Most companies are now facing increased competition from both home and abroad. Product quality, price, delivery, performance and reliability are all of greater importance now than they were last year or the year before. Many industries have moved from an emphasis on production to an emphasis on marketing. In many cases product variety has been increased but often this change has been accompanied by pressures limiting prices and reducing delivery times. These changes have often taken place amidst a climate of deteriorating labour relations, and in the face of labour shortages and increased labour turnover and absenteeism.

Skinner,* examining such problems, has observed that production managers when attempting to deal with the considerable and often conflicting pressures from marketing, engineering, finance, and industrial relations departments often give the impression of being on the defensive, plagued by recurrent crises. Often such crises are very real, and it is barely surprising that practising production managers rarely find time to innovate, develop or refine their practices or concepts.

Until comparatively recently the classification of production systems into mass, batch and jobbing was a realistic concept. Certainly there have always been companies and industries who have operated in the 'grey' areas existing between and around these three categories but nowadays this classification is rapidly becoming largely obsolete. On the one hand there are pressures which are tending to shift jobbing towards batch and batch towards mass production, whilst on the other hand there is a movement in favour of the fragmentation of classical mass-production systems into arrangements more appropriately described as batch production. Indeed, not only is production becoming so complex as to defy the traditional classifications, but also the traditional

* W. Skinner, 'Production under Pressure', *Harvard Business Review*, Vol. 44, No. 6, 1966, pp. 139–46.

foundations or basic principles of production management are now subject to mounting scrutiny and criticism; for example the industrial engineer's principles of work rationalization are no longer considered to be wholly acceptable.

Again referring to Skinner's assessment of the situation, it is abundantly clear that the task of production management is expanding. The production function is no longer subject to the comparatively simple requirements of previous years: to turn out the product in volume at a reasonable quality level, and keep costs down. Far greater demands are now frequently made of production management, for example: 'Make an increasing variety of products, on shorter lead times with smaller runs but with flawless quality. Improve our return on investment by automating and introducing new technology in processes and materials so that we can cut prices to meet local and foreign competition. Mechanize – but keep your schedules flexible, your inventories low, your capital costs minimal, and your work force contented.'

PRODUCTION IN INDUSTRY

The production function is the heart of the industrial enterprise, and accounts for a large proportion of any company's total investment. In the capital goods industries production and product design are the dominant functions. In such industries company growth and profitability depend upon the standards of product design and the efficiency of manufacture. In the consumer goods industries the marketing function often assumes a dominant position as regards managerial and commercial decisions. However, in such industries the investment in production is often at its highest and consequently the importance of the function cannot be underestimated. In fact it is not the relative *importance* of these two functions which differs in different industries, but rather the *initiative* which they exercise in corporate matters.

It has been estimated that approximately one third of all practising managers are engaged in the production function, a figure which is all the more significant when one remembers that there are fewer opportunities for education and training in production management than there are in the financial, personnel and marketing areas.

Normally production managers are persons trained in a subject relevant to the technological environment in which they are working, which means that most managers in the production function are engineers, chemists, or similar specialists and comparatively few are from disciplines such as economics or the behavioural sciences. Such a situation is hardly surprising in view of the manner in which the managerial profession has developed, but it is certainly not the only and not necessarily the best arrangement. Indeed it has been argued that the dominance of technologists in this area is a major reason for the slow development of production management knowledge. Such an argument undoubtedly gains credibility when one considers the position of technologists in the teaching of production management, since it is undoubtedly true that much of the teaching in this subject area has emphasized the importance of the technology to the detriment of the methodology of management. In comparison with other fields of study, little attempt has been made to study production from a conceptual or strategic point of view, and consequently much of the teaching in this area is shallow and narrow.

PRODUCTION IN CONTEXT

Perhaps the principal, initial obstacle to an understanding of the role of production management derives from the rather confusing terminological situation that exists. In particular people have been known to ask how production management differs from or is complemented by industrial engineering and materials management.

Industrial engineering has been defined as 'a broad engineering function that generally involves work measurement, work simplification, statistical quality control, safety program, job evaluation and operations research'.* With the exception of the

* *Encyclopaedic Dictionary of Production and Production Control,* Prentice-Hall, 1964.

inclusion of the last mentioned item, this definition conforms quite closely to the usage the term has acquired in this country, where in general IE has grown out of work study. However, this is not the only definition adopted. The American Institute of Industrial Engineers considers IE to encompass entire responsibility for the design and operation of the production system, a definition which of course approximates to that offered for production management earlier in this book. In some companies the tasks of scheduling, dispatching and progressing of orders are referred to as materials management, the word materials being used to cover raw materials, components, parts and finished products.* Clearly both industrial engineering (narrow and broad definitions) and materials management have something in common with production management. There is undoubtedly some overlap. Industrial engineering may be seen (in this country) as a part of production management, and materials management also as a constituent which further overlaps purchasing and distribution.

Production is the process by which inputs are converted or transformed into outputs. These inputs take the form of resources such as material or labour, whilst the outputs are normally considered to be goods. Production management is therefore concerned with the management (or more specifically the design, construction and operation) of this transformation process.

This definition of production, emphasizing the provision of goods, is synonymous with manufacture. However, as we have previously mentioned, manufacturing is not the only example of an input/transformation/output system, since transformation or conversion processes are also employed to create services. For example, the transformation process is also incorporated in undertakings such as hospitals, libraries, or airlines. Clearly such 'service-creating' systems differ one from another and from manufacture because of their technological characteristics. They are however alike in many respects and especially with regard to their methodologies. In other words the problems associated with the management of these transformation processes are

* H. L. Timms, *The Production Function in Business*, Irwin, 1962.

similar, despite their technological peculiarities and their different objectives. Because of these methodological similarities much of the theory and practice developed for the management of particular types of transformation process is appropriate in the management of the other systems, and vice versa. For this reason the study of the management of such transformation processes is largely independent of the nature of the technology involved.

The recognition of this fact over the last ten years has given rise to two closely associated developments: (1) the redefinition of production management, as the management of systems for the provision of either goods or services, and (2) the establishment of a field of study and practice known as *operations management*, involving the management of all types of transformation process, including manufacture.

The principal advocate of the first development (Starr*) has argued that

the study of production management is quite independent of whatever specific technologies are involved. Methodology overrides the specific technical features of a system. In fact, the strongest methods provide such complete abstraction of any processes that we find ourselves able to consider with equal facility all systems including both real and imaginary ones. Over the years it has also become apparent that input–output systems are remarkably similar when it comes to managing them. There is an underlying pattern that is divisible into some kind of modular units. These can be joined in different ways to form varying configurations of input–output systems. Because of this fact and the characteristic independence of methodology and technology, production management is a cohesive subject . . .

One problem associated with this development is the possibility of creating confusion by redefining a term which is in widespread and largely unquestioned use. It is fortunate, therefore, that the term operations management is now gaining widespread acceptance in business and in education. Operations management is closely related to production management since the production

* M. K. Starr, 'Evolving Concepts in Production Management', Edwin Flippo (ed.), *Proceedings of the 24th Annual Meeting*, Academy of Management, Chicago, 1964, pp. 128–33.

of goods or manufacture is undoubtedly the principal operating system. Operations management therefore connotes a somewhat broader field than production management and embraces the management of transformation systems such as hospitals, public transport, agriculture and libraries, the methodologies of which have a great deal in common despite the obvious differences of their technological configurations.

PRODUCTION MANAGEMENT – THE PRESENT STATE OF KNOWLEDGE

In comparison with other functional subjects the contribution of production to the field of management education is marginal. Much of the present teaching of production management is characterized by an emphasis on analysis rather than synthesis and on tactics rather than strategy. To some extent this situation is inevitable since, because the development of a body of knowledge relevant to production management has depended largely upon the efforts of persons and professions ancillary rather than central to production, the present body of knowledge consists essentially of a collection of discrete contributions. Fortunately the time is now past when production management was considered to consist entirely of important yet intellectually uninspiring tasks such as work study, standardization, variety reduction and so forth. In the more progressive teaching establishments syllabuses have changed radically over the last five or six years, so that present-day courses often bear little or no resemblance to those existing but a short time ago. The present situation, however, leaves a lot to be desired, since at the moment teaching in this area tends to be dominated by attempts to pass on to the student an indication of 'best standard practice' in industry, together with attempts to demonstrate the value and applications of existing techniques in the management of production. Both these objectives can be criticized firstly since practice varies enormously in different firms and industries, and secondly because many currently available techniques are of severely limited value. In fact it can be argued that present practices and techniques are worthy of attention only insofar as an awareness of their limitations indicates the characteristics required of future development.

It is a common misapprehension that continued development in fields such as operational research and computing is reducing the problems of production management. This unfortunately is untrue; indeed it would appear that much of the recent work in operational research has little direct and general application in production management. Certainly many OR investigations have had far-reaching effects in specific production situations but such efforts have done little to accelerate the accumulation of a cohesive body of production-management knowledge. This is not to say that OR techniques (such as those discussed in earlier chapters) and the OR approach to problem-solving is unimportant in production, but rather that techniques, however powerful and however independent of assumptions (and few are), should only be considered as one aspect of the production manager's skills. Computers have had an important effect on production management. The capabilities and opportunities which modern computer systems offer provide a considerable challenge but at the same time they represent a considerable danger, or threat, to production management. The principal value of computers in production management lies in the opportunity they present for the implementation of comprehensive planning and control systems. Herein lies the danger since if such systems are to be designed and used they must of necessity embody presently available knowledge, in the form of decision rules and formulae. In many instances such knowledge is inadequate and we must therefore provide for the modification of these systems when current knowledge is superseded. Without this provision we succeed only in obscuring problems, in perpetuating inefficiency and in stifling initiative for development in this area.

If production management is to continue to develop as a subject or profession, more emphasis must be placed on matters of synthesis since ultimately it is only in their design and construction that production systems are unique. If anything, the recognition of methodological similarities of different types of operating system has encouraged researchers, teachers and practising managers to deal with the components or elements of operating systems. A knowledge of such aspects of systems is 'transferable' but study of the manner in which such elements might be compounded must of necessity be undertaken with only one type of operating system in mind. Attention must now be directed to the nature and characteristics of production systems rather than to the manipulation of the individual elements of such systems. The present preoccupation with the tactics of production management must give way to some extent to the emphasis of strategy. This does not of course imply that elements such as inventory control systems or quality control should be ignored, but merely suggests that the limitations of this approach should be recognized. One cannot reasonably rely solely upon the isolated examination of sub-systems as a means of understanding production unless such systems are truly independent. Unfortunately this condition rarely applies, and consequently it is necessary also to examine the nature of the aggregate production system if worthwhile and generally applicable knowledge is to be gained about its overall design and operation.

This book was written with two objectives in mind. Firstly, it is an attempt to provide a reasonably concise description of the techniques currently available for the analysis of production-management problems. Despite their limitations, many of these techniques are of considerable value and yet they are not as widely used as they might be. The second objective was to attempt to provide a 'base' from which those people involved in the management of production might begin to explore problems of system design. The fact that the need or ability to deal with such problems is as yet largely ignored in both teaching and practice is a barrier to cross in production management. Familiarity with these problems, however, can only follow familiarity with the elements of the systems; the examination of these elements was the principal purpose of this book.

RECOMMENDED READINGS

Production systems and production management, from a Conceptual or System Point of View

Abruzzi, A.,† 'The Production Process: Operating Characteristics', *Management Science*, 11, No. 6, 1965, pp. B.98–118.

Alcalay, J. A., Buffa, E. S.,†§ 'A Proposal for a General Model of a Production System', *International Journal of Production Research*, March 1963.

Skinner, W.,‡ 'Production Under Pressure', *Harvard Business Review*, Nov.–Dec. 1966, pp. 139–46.

Skinner, W., 'Manufacturing – Missing Link in Corporate Strategy', *Harvard Business Review*, May–June 1969, pp. 136–45.

Starr, M. K.,‡§ 'Evolving Concepts in Production Management', Edwin Flippo (ed.), *Proceedings 24th Annual Meeting, Academy of Management*, Chicago 1964.

Thurston, P. H., 'The Concept of a Production System', *Harvard Business Review*, Nov.–Dec., 1965, pp. 70–75.

Timms, H. L., *The Production Function in Business*, Irwin, 1966.

Production Management Methodology and Techniques

1. GENERAL TEXTS

Bowman, E. H., Fetter, R. B., *Analyses for Production and Operations Management*, Irwin, 3rd ed., 1967.

Eilon, S., *Elements of Production Planning and Control*, Macmillan, 1962.

Gavett, J. W., *Production and Operations Management*, Harcourt Brace and World, 1968.

Hanssman, F., *Operations Research in Production and Inventory Control*, Wiley, 1962.

Magee, J. F., Boodman, D. M., *Production Planning and Inventory Control*, McGraw-Hill, 2nd ed. 1969.

Wild, R., *The Techniques of Production Management*, Holt, Rinehart & Winston, 1970.

2. SPECIFIC TOPICS

Bovaird, R. L.,* 'Characteristics of Optimal Maintenance Policies', *Management Science*, April 1961, pp. 238–54.

Conway, R. W.,* 'Priority Dispatching and Work in Progress Inventory in a Job Shop', *Journal of Industrial Engineering*, March–April 1965, pp. 123–30.

242

Durie, F. R. E., 'A Survey of Group Technology and its Potential User Application in the UK', *Production Engineer*, Feb. 1970, pp. 51–61.

Geisler, M. A.,‡ 'A Study of Inventory Theory', *Management Science*, 9, No. 3, 1963, pp. 490–97.

Hertz, D. B.,*‡ 'Risk Analysis in Capital Investment', *Harvard Business Review*, 42, No. 1, Jan.–Feb. 1964, pp. 95–106.

Ignall, E. G.,*‡ 'A Review of Assembly Line Balancing', *Journal of Industrial Engineering*, Vol. 16, No. 4, 1965, pp. 244–54.

Le Grande, E., 'The Development of a Factory Simulation Using Actual Operating Data', *Management Technology*, Vol. 3, No. 1, May 1963.

Magee, J. F.,‡ 'Decision Trees for Decision Making', *Harvard Business Review*, 42, 4, July–Aug. 1964, pp. 126–38.

Moodie, C. L., Novotny, D. J., 'Computer Scheduling and Control Systems for Discrete Part Manufacture', *Journal of Industrial Engineering*, Vol. 19, No. 7, 1968, pp. 336–41.

Moore, J. M., Wilson, R. C., 'A Review of Simulation Research in Job Shop Scheduling', *Production and Inventory Management*, Jan. 1967, pp. 1–10.

Turban, E., 'The Line of Balance – a Management by Exception Tool', *Journal of Industrial Engineering*, Vol. 19, No. 9, 1968.

Vaill, P. B.,‡ 'Industrial Engineering and Socio-Technical Systems', *Journal of Industrial Engineering*, Vol. 16, No. 9, 1967, pp. 530–38.

Wiest, J. D.,‡ 'Heuristic Programs for Decision Making', *Harvard Business Review*, 44, No. 5, Sept.–Oct. 1966, pp. 129–43.

* These articles are reprinted in Hottenstein, *Models and Analysis for Production Management*, International, Scranton, Penn., 1968.

† These articles are reprinted in Buffa, E. S. (ed.), *Readings in Production and Operations Management*, Wiley, 1966.

‡ These articles are reprinted in Groff, G. K., Muth, J. F. (eds.), *Operations Management – Selected Readings*, Irwin, 1969.

§ These articles are reprinted in Starr, M. K. (ed.), *Management of Production*, Penguin, 1970.

Index

MORE ABOUT PENGUINS
AND PELICANS

Penguinews, which appears every month, contains details of all the new books issued by Penguins as they published. From time to time it is supplemented by *Penguins in Print*, which is a complete list of all available books published by Penguins. (There are well over three thousand of these.)

A specimen copy of *Penguinews* will be sent to you free on request, and you can become a subscriber for the price of the postage. For a year's issues (including the complete lists) please send 30p if you live in the United Kingdom, or 60p if you live elsewhere. Just write to Dept EP, Penguin Books Ltd, Harmondsworth, Middlesex, enclosing a cheque or postal order, and your name will be added to the mailing list.

Note: *Penguinews* and *Penguins in Print* are not available in the U.S.A. or Canada

MANAGEMENT DECISIONS
AND THE ROLE OF FORECASTING

JAMES MORRELL

Forecasting in business, though notably more sophisticated than crystal-gazing, is still an art rather than a science because of the imperfection of past statistics and our continuing ignorance of the future. The business wizard of today is the man who can, as scientifically as possible, lessen the uncertainties of the future and pinpoint the risks, whether at company or national level.

This Pelican is a guide, prepared by a specialist of more than twenty years' experience, to business forecasting in all its aspects and the role it fulfils for management. A team of economists engaged on the production of *Framework Forecasts* contribute articles on the national economy, the balance of payments and future government policy, trends in major industries, public spending and interest rates and, at the more workaday level of the individual company, show how forecasts are made of costs, prices, sales and profits.

With the aid of forty charts the book explains the different techniques for forecasting, the basic information required, and the ways in which findings can be interpreted.

Pelican Library of Business and Management

AN INSIGHT INTO
MANAGEMENT ACCOUNTING

JOHN SIZER

'John Sizer has attempted to write a comprehensive work on company finance, which should be intelligible to the general executive. It is certainly an impressively relevant book, with numerous practical examples of such concepts as capital investment appraisal, marginal costing, and budgetary control' – *Financial Times*

'. . . for managers and management students rather than professional accountants. The author explains the elements of financial and cost accounting and goes on to consider financial planning, investment appraisal, budgetary control and decision making. . . . The text is illustrated by diagrams and examples and numerous references are cited. This is no easy popularization but a substantial contribution to an important subject' – *The Times Educational Supplement*

'The book cannot be too strongly recommended, and its cost is minimal' – *Management Accounting*

'If you feel your managing director does not understand you, send him a copy in a plain envelope' – *Accountant's Magazine*

Professor Sizer's book headed the paperback section of the Metra best-sellers' list of management books for the first nine months of 1970.

Pelican Library of Business and Management

COMPUTERS, MANAGERS
AND SOCIETY

MICHAEL ROSE

'Here is a book on computers and computer technology written by a sociologist, and it is one of the very few which sets out clearly, simply and, even more important, objectively what computers are all about. It is also amusing . . .' – *New Society*

After a general survey of the development of computer-controlled data processing, Michael Rose examines the complex effects of the computer upon the clerical worker – the new opportunities, the dangers of alienation, the threat of technological unemployment. He then focuses upon the fast-developing problems of managers. Many of the standard managerial functions can already be programmed. But should executives delegate qualitative decisions to a machine? And if so, how far can and should these changes go?

'Computerization' presents managers with new opportunities on a structural scale unmatched since the Industrial Revolution. Do they really understand the new situation? Can they, when it is transforming itself so rapidly? And are we enough aware of the effects of the computer upon an even larger social group – society itself – now faced with the need to clarify its whole attitude to technological change?

'Knowledgeable, intelligent and clearly written' – *The Times Literary Supplement*